The
Economist

Style Guide

11th Edition

PUBLICAFFAIRS
New York

Typeset in EcoType by MacGuru Ltd
info@macguru.org.uk

Library of Congress Control Number: 2015936805
ISBN 978-1-61039-538-0 (PB)
ISBN 978-1-61039-575-5 (EB)

First Edition

10 9 8 7 6 5 4 3 2 1

Contents

Preface

Every newspaper has its own style book, a set of rules telling journalists whether to write e-mail or email, Gadaffi or Qaddafi, judgement or judgment. *The Economist's* style book does this and a bit more. It also warns writers of some common mistakes and encourages them to write with clarity and simplicity.

All the prescriptive judgments in the style guide are directly derived from those used each week in writing and editing *The Economist.*

This eleventh edition of the "The Economist Style Guide" is in three parts. The first is based on the style book used by those who edit *The Economist;* it is largely the work of John Grimond, who over the years was editor of the Britain, United States and Foreign sections, before retiring in 2013. Johnny is a hard act to follow, and he left at a time when proper English usage seemed in full retreat in the face of texting, Tweeting and internet jargon generally. His work still stands as a bulwark against it, as well as a monument to his impish wit and his sense of euphony, rightness and correctness. If slight cracks have now appeared in the bulwark, it is because language is a living thing that continually changes; some changes are benign, and some (such as the pervasive "smartness" of the digital age) simply cannot be resisted.

The second part of the book, on American and British English, describes some of the main differences between the two great English-speaking areas in spelling, grammar and usage.

To make the style guide of greater general interest, Part 3 consists of handy reference material that might appeal to readers of *The Economist.*

Throughout the text, italic type is used for examples except where they are presented in lists, when the type is roman, as this text is. Words in **bold** indicate a separate but relevant entry, that is, a cross-reference. Small capitals are used only in the way *The Economist* uses them, for which see the entry **abbreviations**.

Many people have been involved in this book as it has developed and changed over the years. Thanks are due to all of them, with special thanks to Penny Butler, Ingrid Esling, Graham Douglas and Penny Garrett, whose help has been invaluable and continues to be so.

Ann Wroe,
Obituaries Editor, *The Economist*
March 2015

Introduction

On only two scores can *The Economist* hope to outdo its rivals consistently. One is the quality of its analysis; the other is the quality of its writing. The aim of this book is to give some general advice on writing, to point out some common errors and to set some arbitrary rules.

The first requirement of *The Economist* is that it should be readily understandable. Clarity of writing usually follows clarity of thought. So think what you want to say, then say it as simply as possible. Keep in mind George Orwell's six elementary rules:

1 Never use a **metaphor**, simile or other figure of speech which you are used to seeing in print (*see* **metaphors**).
2 Never use a long word where a short one will do (*see* **short words**).
3 If it is possible to cut out a word, always cut it out (*see* **unnecessary words**).
4 Never use the passive where you can use the active (*see* **grammar and syntax**).
5 Never use a foreign phrase, a scientific word or a jargon word if you can think of an everyday English equivalent.
6 Break any of these rules sooner than say anything outright barbarous.

Readers are primarily interested in what you have to say. By the way in which you say it, you may encourage them either to read on or to give up. If you want them to read on:

Catch the attention of the reader and then get straight into the article. Do not spend several sentences clearing your throat, setting the scene or sketching in the background. Introduce the facts as you tell the story and hold the reader by the way you unfold the tale and by a fresh but unpretentious use of language.

In starting your article, let your model be the essays of Francis Bacon. He starts "Of Riches" with "I cannot call riches better than the baggage of virtue." "Of Cunning" opens with "We take cunning for a sinister or crooked wisdom." "Of Suspicion" is instantly on the wing with "Suspicions amongst thoughts are like bats amongst birds, they ever fly by twilight." Each of these beginnings carries implicitly within it an entire essay. Each seizes the reader by the lapels and at once draws him into the subject. No gimmickry is needed, no flowery language, no literary contrivance. Plain words on their own carry enough meaning to provoke an intriguing thought, stir the reader's curiosity and thus make him want to continue.

You must strive for a similar effect. Articles in *The Economist* should be like essays, in that they have a beginning, a middle and an end. They should not be mere bits of information stitched together. Each should be a coherent whole, a series of paragraphs that follow logically in order and, ideally, will suffer if even one sentence is cut out. If the article is a report, the facts must be selected and presented as a story. If it is a leader or more analytical article, it should also have a sense of sequence, so that the reader feels he is progressing from a beginning to a conclusion.

Either way, it is up to you to provide the ideas, analysis and argument that bind the elements of the article together. That is the hard part. Once you have them, though, you need only plain, straightforward words to express them. Do not imagine that you can disguise the absence of thought with long words, stale metaphors or the empty jargon of academics. In moderation, however, you can enliven your writing with a fresh metaphor, an occasional exuberance or an unusual word or phrase that nicely suits your purpose.

Read through your writing several times. Edit it ruthlessly, whether by cutting or polishing or sharpening, on each occasion. Avoid repetition. Cut out anything superfluous. And resist any temptation to achieve a literary effect by making elliptical remarks or allusions to unexplained people or events. Rather, hold your reader's attention by keeping the story moving. If the tale begins to flag, or the arguments seem less than convincing, you can rescue it only by the sharpness of your mind. Nothing is to be gained by resorting to orotundities and grandiloquence, still less by calling on clichés and vogue expressions. Unadorned, unfancy prose is usually all you need.

Do not be stuffy. "To write a genuine, familiar or truly English style", said Hazlitt, "is to write as anyone would speak in common conversation who had a thorough command or choice of words or who could discourse with ease, force and perspicuity setting aside all pedantic and oratorical flourishes."

Use the language of everyday speech, not that of spokesmen, lawyers or bureaucrats (so prefer *let* to *permit*, *people* to *persons*, *buy* to *purchase*, *colleague* to *peer*, *way out* to *exit*, *present* to *gift*, *rich* to *wealthy*, *show* to *demonstrate*, *break* to *violate*). Pomposity and long-windedness tend to obscure meaning, or reveal the lack of it: strip them away in favour of plain words.

Do not be hectoring or arrogant. Those who disagree with you are not necessarily *stupid* or *insane*. Nobody needs to be described as silly: let your analysis show that he is. When you express opinions, do not simply make assertions. The aim is not just to tell readers what you think, but to persuade them; if you use arguments, reasoning and evidence, you may succeed. Go easy on the *oughts* and *shoulds*.

Do not be too pleased with yourself. Don't boast of your own cleverness by telling readers that you correctly predicted something or that you have a scoop. You are more likely to bore or irritate them than to impress them.

Do not be too chatty. *Surprise, surprise* is more irritating than informative. So is *Ho, ho* and, in the middle of a sentence, *wait for it*, etc.

Do not be too didactic. If too many sentences begin *Compare, Consider, Expect, Imagine, Look at, Note, Prepare for, Remember* or *Take*, readers will think they are reading a textbook (or, indeed, a style book). This may not be the way to persuade them to renew their subscriptions.

Do your best to be lucid. ("I see but one rule: to be clear", Stendhal.) Simple sentences help. Keep complicated constructions and gimmicks to a minimum, if necessary by remembering the *New Yorker*'s comment: "Backward ran sentences until reeled the mind."

Mark Twain described how a good writer treats sentences: "At times he may indulge himself with a long one, but he will make sure there are no folds in it, no vaguenesses, no parenthetical interruptions of its view as a whole; when he has done with it, it won't be a sea-serpent with half of its arches under the water; it will be a torch-light procession."

Long paragraphs, like long sentences, can confuse the reader. "The paragraph", according to Fowler, "is essentially a unit of thought, not of length; it must be homogeneous in subject matter and sequential in treatment." One-sentence paragraphs should be used only occasionally.

Clear thinking is the key to clear writing. "A scrupulous writer", observed Orwell, "in every sentence that he writes will ask himself at least four questions, thus: What am I trying to say? What words will express it? What image or idiom will make it clearer? Is this image fresh enough to have an effect? And he will probably ask himself two more: Could I put it more shortly? Have I said anything that is avoidably ugly?"

Scrupulous writers will also notice that their copy is edited only lightly and is likely to be used. It may even be read.

part 1

The essence of style

a or the *see* grammar and syntax.

abbreviations

Write words in their full form on first appearance:
Trades Union Congress (not TUC), *Troubled Asset Relief Programme* (not TARP)
unless an abbreviation or acronym is so familiar that it is used more often in full:
AIDS BBC CIA EU FBI HIV IMF NATO NGO OECD UNESCO
or unless the full form would provide little illumination –
AWACS, DNA. If in doubt about its familiarity, explain what the organisation is or does. After the first mention, try not to repeat the abbreviation too often; so write *the agency* rather than the IAEA, *the party* rather than the KMT, to avoid spattering the page with capital letters. And prefer *chief executive, boss* or *manager* to CEO.

There is no need to give the initials of an organisation if it is not referred to again. This clutters both the page and the brain.

Do not use spatterings of abbreviations and acronyms simply in order to cram more words in; you will end up irritating readers rather than informing them. An article in a recent issue of *The Economist* contained the following:
CIA DCI DNI DOD DVD FBI NCTC NSA

Some of these are well known to most readers and can readily be held in the mind. But unfamiliar abbreviations may oblige the reader to constantly refer back to the first use.

ampersands should be used:

1   when they are part of the name of a company:
    Procter & Gamble Pratt & Whitney
2   for such things as constituencies, where two names are
    linked to form one unit:
    *The rest of Brighouse & Spenborough joins with the Batley part
    of Batley & Morley to form Batley & Spen.*
    *The area thus became the Pakistani province of Kashmir and the
    Indian state of Jammu & Kashmir.*
3   in R&D and S&1.

definite article If an abbreviation can be pronounced – COSATU,
NATO, UNESCO – it does not generally require the definite
article. Other organisations, except companies, should usually be
preceded by the:
the BBC *the* KGB *the* NHS *the* NIESR *the* UNHCR

elements do not take small caps when abbreviated:
carbon dioxide is CO_2
lead is Pb
methane is CH_4

However:
chlorofluorocarbons are CFCS
the oxides of nitrogen are generally NOX

Different isotopes of the same element are distinguished by
raised (superscript) prefixes:
carbon-14 is ^{14}C
helium-3 is ^3He

Do not sprinkle chemical symbols unnecessarily: they may
put readers off. But common abbreviations such as CO_2 may
sometimes be used for variety.

headings, cross-heads, captions, etc In headings, rubrics, cross-
heads, footnotes, captions, tables, charts (including sources), use
ordinary caps, not small caps.

initials in people's and companies' names take points (with a

space between initials and name, but not between initials). In general, follow the practice preferred by people, companies and organisations in writing their own names, for example:
I.M. Pei J.C. Penney J. Sainsbury A.N. Wilson

junior and senior Spell out in full (and lower case) junior and senior after a name:
George Bush junior   George Bush senior

lower case Abbreviate:
kilograms *(not* kilogrammes*)* to kg (or kilos)
kilometres per hour to kph
kilometres to km
miles per hour to mph

Use lower case for *kg, km, lb* (never *lbs*), *mph* and other measures, and for *ie, eg; ie* should be followed by a comma. When used with figures, these lower-case abbreviations should follow immediately, with no space:
11am 4.30pm 15kg 35mm 100mph 78rpm

Two abbreviations together, however, must be separated: *60m b/d.* Use *b/d* not *bpd* as an abbreviation for *barrels per day.*

MPS Except in British contexts, use MP only after first spelling out member of Parliament in full (in many places an MP is a military policeman).
Members of the *European Parliament* are MEPS (not Euro-MPS).
Members of the *Scottish Parliament* are MSPS.
Members of the *Welsh Assembly* are AMS (Assembly Members).

organisations
EFTA is the European Free Trade Association.
The FAO is the Food and Agriculture Organisation.
The FDA is the Food and Drug Administration.
The IDA is the International Development Association.
NAFTA is the North American Free-Trade Agreement.
The PLO is the Palestine Liberation Organisation.

pronounceable abbreviations

Abbreviations that can be pronounced and are composed of bits of words rather than just initials should be spelt out in upper and lower case:

Cocom	Mercosur	Unicef
Frelimo	Nepad	Unisom
Kfor	Renamo	Unprofor
Legco	Sfor	

There is generally no need for more than one initial capital letter, unless the word is a name: *ConsGold, KwaZulu, McKay, MiG*.

ranks and titles Do not use *Prof, Sen, Col*, etc. *Lieut-Colonel* and *Lieut-Commander* are permissible. So is *Rev*, but it must be preceded by *the* and followed by a Christian name or initial: *the Rev Jesse Jackson* (thereafter *Mr Jackson*).

scientific units named after individuals Scientific units, except those of temperature, that are named after individuals are not capitalised when written out in full: *watt, joule*, etc. When abbreviated these units should be set in small capitals, though any attachments denoting multiples go in lower case:

watt is w
kilowatt, 1,000 watts, is kw
milliwatt, one-thousandth of a watt, is mw
megawatt, 1m watts, is mw
gigawatt, 1 billion (10^9) watts, is gw
terawatt, 1 trillion (10^{12}) watts, is tw
petawatt, 1 quadrillion (10^{15}) watts, is pw
megahertz is mhz

small caps usage

In body text, use small capitals for abbreviations, acronyms and proper names spelt in capitals, whether they can be pronounced as words or not, with no points:

cif eu fob gdp ikea nato

Single letters, when attached by hyphens to words, should also generally be set in small caps:

a-level b-grade t-shirt u-turn x-ray y chromosome

Abbreviations that include upper-case and lower-case letters must be set in a mixture of small capitals and lower case: BPhil, BSkyB, PhD. The same rule applies if an abbreviation is linked to a number: AK-47, MiG-25, M1, SALT-2.

Brackets, apostrophes and all other typographical furniture accompanying small capitals, including the plural and genitive s, are not set in small capitals: IOUs, MPs' *salaries*, SDRs, etc.

Do not use small caps for:
the elements of the periodic table, eg *H, Pb, Sn, NaCl*
degrees of temperature, eg °C, °F, °R
currencies, eg *NKr, SFr*
roman numerals, eg *C, D, I, L, M, V, X.* So *Richard III, Louis XIV, Pope John XXIII* and so on. But do not adorn popes, monarchs, etc, with numerical postscripts unless they are needed to differentiate, for example, Benedict XVI from Benedict XV, or Elizabeth II from her 16th-century namesake.
anything in captions, charts (including sources), footnotes, headings, rubrics or tables

writing out upper-case abbreviations Most upper-case abbreviations are shortenings of proper names with initial capital letters. The LSO is the *London Symphony Orchestra*. However, there are exceptions:
CAP *but* common agricultural policy
EMU *but* economic and monetary union
GDP *but* gross domestic product
PSBR *but* public-sector borrowing requirement
VLSI *but* very large-scale integration

miscellaneous Spell out:
page pages hectares miles

Remember, too, that the *v* of HIV stands for virus, so do not write HIV *virus*.

See **measures** in Part 3.

absent In Latin *absent* is a verb meaning *they are away*. In English it is either an adjective (*absent friends*) or a verb (*to absent yourself*).

It is not a preposition meaning *in the absence of*.

accents On words now accepted as English, use accents only when they make a crucial difference to pronunciation:
café cliché communiqué éclat exposé façade soupçon
But: *chateau decor elite feted naive*

The main accents and diacritical signs are:

acute	république
grave	grand-mère
circumflex	bête noire
umlaut	Länder, Österreich (Austria)
cedilla	français
tilde	señor, São Paulo

If you use one accent (except the tilde – strictly, a diacritical sign), use all:
émigré mêlée protégé résumé

Put the accents and diacritical signs on French, German, Spanish and Portuguese names and words only:

José Manuel Barroso	cafèzinho
Federico Peña	coñac
Françoise de Panafieu	déjeuner
Wolfgang Schäuble	Frühstück

Any foreign word in italics should, however, be given its proper accents. *See also* **italics**.

acronym A pronounceable word, formed from the initials of other words, like *radar, nimby* or NATO. It is not a set of initials, like the BBC or the IMF.

actionable means *giving ground for a lawsuit*. Do not use it to mean *susceptible of being put into practice*: prefer *practical* or *practicable*. Do not use *action* as a verb.

adjectives and adverbs *see* **grammar and syntax, punctuation.**

adjectives of proper nouns *see* **grammar and syntax, punctuation.**

address What did journalists and politicians do in the days, not so long ago, when *address* was used as a verb only before objects such as *audience, letter, ball, haggis* and, occasionally, *themselves*? Questions can be *answered*, issues *discussed*, problems *solved*, difficulties *dealt with*. *See* **clichés.**

aetiology is the *science of causation*, or *an inquiry into something's origins. Etiolate is to make or become pale for lack of light.*

affect (verb) means to have an influence on, as in *the novel affected his attitude to immigrants. See also* **effect.**

affirmative action is a euphemism, uglier even than *human-rights abuses* and more obscure even than *comfort station*, with little to be said for it. It is too late to suppress it altogether and perhaps too soon to consign it to the midden of civil-rights studies, but try to avoid it as much as possible. If you cannot escape it, put it in quotation marks on first mention and, unless the context makes its meaning clear, explain what it is. You may, however, find that *preferential treatment, job preferment* or even *discrimination* serve just as well as alternatives. *See* **euphemisms.**

affordable By whom? Avoid *affordable housing, affordable computers* and other unthinking uses of advertising lingo.

Afghan names *see* **names.**

aggravate means *make worse*, not *irritate* or *annoy*.

aggression is an unattractive quality, so do not call a *keen* salesman an *aggressive* one (unless his foot is in the door).

agony column Remember that when Sherlock Holmes perused this, it was a *personal column*. Only recently has it come to mean *letters to an agony aunt*.

agree Things are agreed *on, to* or *about*, not just agreed.

aircraft *see* **hyphens** and **italics.**

alibi An *alibi* is the fact of being elsewhere, not a false explanation.

alternate, alternative *Alternate* (as an adjective) means *every other*. As a noun, it has now come to mean a *stand-in* for a director or delegate. *Alternative* (as a noun), strictly, means one of two, not one of three, four, five or more (which may be *options*). As an adjective, *alternative* means *of two* (*or, loosely, more*) *things*, or *possible as an alternative*.

Americanisms

See Chapter 2, on British and American usage. To the points made there might be added the following preferred usages in British English (and in *The Economist*):
and *not* additionally
the army *not* the military (noun)
car *not* automobile
company *not* corporation
court *not* courtroom or courthouse
district *not* neighborhood
normality *not* normalcy
oblige *not* obligate
rocket *not* skyrocket

Back-formations are common in English, so *curate*, the verb meaning *organise* or *superintend* exhibitions of pictures, sculptures and so on formed from *curator*, is now acceptable in British English. But it is still too soon for *gallerist* (prefer *dealer* or, if appropriate, just *gallery*).

adverbs Put adverbs where you would put them in normal speech, which is usually after the verb (not before it, which usually is where Americans put them).

avoiding nouning adjectives Similarly, do not noun adjectives such as:
advisory – prefer warning
centennial – prefer centenary
inaugural – prefer inauguration
meet (noun) – *meeting* is better
spend (noun) – *spending* is preferable

avoiding verbing and adjectiving nouns Try not to verb nouns or to adjective them. So do not:
access files (except electronically)
action proposals
author books (still less *co-author* them)
critique style guides
gun someone down; use *shoot*
haemorrhage red ink (haemorrhage is a noun)
let one event *impact* another
loan money
pressure colleagues (*press* will do)
progress reports
source inputs
trial programmes

Avoid *parenting* (or using the word) and *parenting skills*. (*See also* **grammar and syntax.**)

And though it is sometimes necessary to use nouns as adjectives, there is no need to call:
an *attempted coup* a *coup attempt*
a *suspected terrorist* a *terrorist suspect*
the *Californian legislature* the *California legislature*

Vilest of all is the habit of throwing together several nouns into one ghastly adjectival reticule:
Texas millionaire real-estate developer and failed thrift entrepreneur Hiram Turnipseed ...

coining words Avoid coining verbs and adjectives unnecessarily. Instead of:
dining experiences and *writing experiences*: use *dining* and *writing*
downplaying criticism, you can *play* it *down* (or perhaps *minimise* it)
upcoming and *ongoing* are better put as *forthcoming* and *continuing*
Why *outfit* your children when you can *fit* them *out*?

Hosting has now entered the language (often to mean *acting as host at an event paid for by someone else*, otherwise giving would be the right word), but *guesting* (*appearing as a guest* on a programme) should be kept at bay.

overuse of American words Do not feel obliged to follow American fashion in overusing such words as:
constituency – try *supporters*
gubernatorial – this means *relating to a governor*
perception – try *belief* or *view*
rhetoric (of which there is too little, not too much) – try *language* or *speeches* or *exaggeration* if that is what you mean

In Britain:
Cars are *hired*, not *rented*, and are left in *car parks*, not *parking lots*.
City centres are not central cities.
Companies: *call for* a record profit if you wish to exhort the workers, but not if you merely predict one. And do not *post* it if it has been achieved. If it has not, look for someone new to *head*, not *head up*, the company.
Countries, nations and states: London is the *country*'s capital, not the *nation*'s. If you wish to build a *nation*, you will *bind its peoples together*; if you wish to build a *state*, you will forge its *institutions*.
Deep: make a *deep* study or even a study *in depth*, but not an *in-depth* study.
Ex-servicemen are not necessarily *veterans*.
Football for most people is a *game* – you do not have to call it a *sport* – that Americans call *soccer*.
Do not *figure out* if you can *work out*.
Fresh should be used of vegetables, not teenagers.
Grow a beard or a tomato but not a company (or indeed a salesman: the *Financial Times* reported on August 8th 2003 that BMW was "to grow its own car salesmen").
Hikes are walks, not increases.
Do not use *likely* to mean *probably*.
Make a *rumpus* rather than a *ruckus*, and *snigger* rather than *snicker*.
On-site inspections are allowed, but not *on-train* teams or *in-ear* headphones.

15

Outside America, nowadays, you stay *outside* the door, not
outside of it.

Programme: you may *program* a computer, but in all other
contexts the word is *programme*.

Use *power cut* or *blackout* rather than *outage*.

Keep a promise, rather than *deliver on* it.

Raise cattle and pigs, but children are (or should be) *brought up*.

Regular is not a synonym for *ordinary* or *normal*: Mussolini
brought in the *regular* train, All-Bran the *regular* man; it is quite
normal to be without either.

A *religious group* sounds better than a *faith-based organisation*.

Scenarios are best kept for the theatre, *postures* for the gym,
parameters for the parabola.

Do not *task* people, or *meet with* them.

Throw *stones*, not *rocks*.

Trains run from *railway stations*, not *train stations*. The people in
them, and on buses, are *passengers*, not *riders*.

Use *senior* rather than *ranking*.

And only the speechless are *dumb* and the insane *mad*.

tenses Choose tenses according to British usage, too. In
particular, do not fight shy – as Americans often do – of the
perfect tense, especially where no date or time is given. Thus:
Mr Obama has woken up to the danger is preferable to *Mr Obama
woke up to the danger*, unless you can add *last week* or *when he
heard the explosion*.

Do not write *Your salary just got smaller* or *I shrunk the kids*. In
British English *Your salary has just got smaller* and *I've shrunk the
kids*.

See also **adjectives of proper nouns, euphemisms, grammar and
syntax**, and Part 2.

among and between Some sticklers insist that, where division
is involved, *among* should be used where three or more are
concerned, *between* where only two are concerned. So:
*The plum jobs were shared among the Socialists, the Liberals and
the Christian Democrats, while the president and the vice-president
divided the cash between themselves.*

This distinction is unnecessary. But take care with *between*. *To fall between two stools*, however painful, is grammatically acceptable; *to fall between the cracks* is to challenge the laws of physics.

Prefer *among* to *amongst*.

an should be used before a word beginning with a vowel sound (*an egg, an umbrella, an MP*) or an h if, and only if, the h is silent (*an honorary degree*). But *a European, a university, a U-turn, a hospital, a hotel. Historical* is an exception: it is preceded by *an*, the h remaining silent.

anarchy means the *complete absence of law or government*. It may be harmonious or chaotic.

animals For the spelling of the Latin names of animals, plants, etc, *see* **Latin names**.

annus horribilis, annus mirabilis *Annus horribilis* is often used, presumably in contrast to *annus mirabilis*, to describe an *awful year*, for example by Queen Elizabeth in 1992 (the year of her daughter's divorce, the separation of the Duke and Duchess of York and a fire at Windsor Castle). It serves its purpose well, but it should be noted that *annus mirabilis* originally meant much the same thing: 1666, of which it was first used, was the year of the great fire of London and the second year of the great plague in England. Physicists, however, have latterly used the term to describe 1932, the year in which the neutron was discovered, the positron identified and the atomic nucleus first broken up artificially. And Philip Larkin, more understandably, used it to describe 1963, the year in which sexual intercourse began.

anon means *soon*, though it once meant *straight away*. *Presently* also means *soon*, though it is increasingly misused to mean *now*. (*See also* **presently**.)

anticipate does not mean *expect*. It means to forestall or look forward to. Jack and Jill expected to marry; if they anticipated marriage, only Jill might find herself expectant.

apostasy, heresy If you abandon your religion, you commit *apostasy*. If that religion is the prevailing one in your community and your beliefs are contrary to its orthodoxy, you commit *heresy*.

apostrophes *see* **punctuation**.

appeal is intransitive nowadays (except in America), so appeal *against decisions*.

appraise means *set a price on. Apprise* means *inform*.

Arabic The Arabic alphabet has several consonants that have no exact equivalents in English: for example, a hard *t* as well as a normal soft one, a hard *s* as well as a soft one, two different (one vocalised, the other not) *th* sounds. Moreover, there are three sounds: a glottal stop like a hiccup, a glottal sound akin to strangulation and a uvular trill. Ultra-fastidious transliterators try to reproduce these subtleties with a profusion of apostrophes and *hs* which yield spellings like Mu'ammar al-Qadhdhafi. The risk of error and the sheer ugliness on the page are too great to justify the effort, so usually ignore the differences.

Vowels present a lesser problem. There are only three – *a*, *u*, *i* – but each can be lengthened. Do not bother to differentiate between the short and the long *a*. Occasionally, a spelling is established where the *u* has been lengthened by using *oo*, as in *Sultan Qaboos*. In such instances, follow that convention, but in general go for *ou*, as in *murabitoun* or *Ibn Khaldoun*. For a long *i* you should normally use *ee* (as in *mujahideen*).

Muhammad is the correct spelling unless it is part of the name of someone who spells it differently. (*See also* **names**.)

as of say, April 5th or April. Prefer *on* (or *after*, or *since*) April 5th, in April.

assassinate is, properly, the term used not just for any old killing, but for the murder of a prominent person, usually for a political purpose. (*See* **execute**.)

as to There is usually a more appropriate preposition, eg *about*. Or rewrite the sentence.

autarchy, autarky *Autarchy* means absolute sovereignty. *Autarky* means self-sufficiency.

avert, avoid, evade To *avert* something means to head it off. To *avoid* it means to keep away from it. To *evade* it means to elude it or escape it artfully. Tax *avoidance* is legal; tax *evasion* is not.

avocation An *avocation* is a distraction or *diversion from your ordinary employment*, not a synonym for *vocation*.

bail, bale In the hayfield, *bale*; otherwise *bail, bail out* and *bail-out* (noun).

Bangladeshi names *see* **names.**

-based A *Paris-based group* may be all right, if, say, that group operates abroad (otherwise just say a *group in Paris*). But avoid *community-based, faith-based, knowledge-based*, etc. A *community-based organisation* is perhaps a *community organisation*; a *faith-based organisation* is probably a *church*; a *knowledge-based industry* needs explanation: all industries depend on knowledge.

beg the question means neither *raise the question, invite the question* nor *evade the answer*. To *beg the question* is to adopt an argument whose conclusion depends upon assuming the truth of the very conclusion the argument is designed to produce.
All governments should promote free trade because otherwise protectionism will increase. This begs the question.

Belarusian names *see* **names.**

bellwether This is the leading sheep of a flock, on whose neck a bell is hung. It has nothing to do with climate, prevailing winds or the like, but the term is used in the stockmarket.

between *see* **among and between.**

biannual, biennial *Biannual* can mean twice a year or once every two years. Avoid. Since *biennial* also means once every two years, that is best avoided too. So are *bimonthly* and *biweekly*, which also have two meanings. Luckily, *fortnightly* is unambiguous.

bicentennial Prefer bicentenary (as a noun).

black *In the black* means *in profit* in Britain, but *making losses* in some places. Use *in profit.*

blond, blonde *Blond* is an adjective and, unusually, in its adjectival use it retains its two genders (see **grammar and syntax,** masculine or feminine). Use *blonde* as a noun, referring to a woman with blond hair: *the blonde in the corner of the room.* Use *blond* for everything else, including the hair of a blonde.

blooded, bloodied *Blooded* means *pedigreed* (as in *blue-blooded*) or *initiated. Bloodied* means *wounded.*

bon vivant not *bon viveur.*

born, borne are both past participles of the verb *bear. Born* is used in the sense of giving birth: *She was born in April. Borne* is used for *supporting* or *putting up with* (*The victims had borne enough pain*) and for giving birth in active constructions (*She had already borne six children*).

both ... and A preposition placed after *both* should be repeated after *and.* Thus *both to right and to left;* but *to both right and left* is all right.

brackets *see* **punctuation.**

British titles *see* **titles.**

brokerage is what a stockbroking firm does, not what it is.

C

cadre Keep this word for the *framework of a military unit* or the *officers of such a unit*, not for a *communist functionary*.

calibres *see* **hyphens**.

Cambodian names *see* **names**.

Canute's exercise on the seashore was designed to persuade his courtiers of what he knew to be true but they doubted, ie, that he was not omnipotent. Don't imply he was surprised to get his feet wet.

capitals A balance has to be struck between so many capitals that the eyes dance and so few that the reader is diverted more by our style than by our substance. The general rule is to dignify with capital letters organisations and institutions, but not people; and full names, but not informal ones. More exact rules are laid out below. Even these, however, leave some decisions to individual judgment. If in doubt use lower case unless it looks absurd. And remember that "a foolish consistency is the hobgoblin of little minds" (Ralph Waldo Emerson).

avoiding confusion Use capitals to avoid confusion, especially with no (and therefore yes). *In Bergen no votes predominated* suggests a stalemate, whereas *In Bergen No votes predominated* suggests a triumph of noes over yeses. In most contexts, though, yes and no should be lower case: "*The answer is no.*"

cities *City* with a capital, even though *City* is not an integral part of their names:

Guatemala City   New York City
Ho Chi Minh City   Panama City
Kuwait City   Quebec City
Mexico City

City also takes a capital when it is part of the name:

Dodge City   Quezon City
Kansas City   Salt Lake City
Oklahoma City

compass points Lower case for:
east west north south
except when part of a name (*North Korea, South Africa, West End*) or part of a thinking group: *the South, the Midwest, the West* (but lower case for vaguer areas such as the American *north-east, north-west, south-east, south-west*). Lower-case too for the adjectives: *midwestern, western, southern.*

The regions of Africa are *southern, east, west* and *north Africa*. But *South Africa* is the name of the country.

Europe Europe's divisions are no longer neatly political, and are now geographically imprecise, so use lower case for central, eastern and western Europe.

Use *West Germany* (*West Berlin*) and *East Germany* (*East Berlin*) only in historical references. They are now *west* or *western Germany* (*Berlin*) and *east* or *eastern Germany* (*eastern Berlin*).

The *Basque country* (or *region*) is ill-defined and contentious, and may include parts of both France and Spain, so lower case for country (or region).

See also **Euro-.**

finance In finance there are particular exceptions to the general rule of initial capitals for full names, lower case for informal ones. There are also rules about what to do on second mention.

Deutschmarks are still known just as *D-marks*, even though all references are historical.

Special drawing rights are lower case but are abbreviated as SDRs, except when used with a figure as a currency (SDR500m).

The *Bank of England* and its foreign equivalents have initial caps when named formally and separately, but collectively they are central banks in lower case, except those like Brazil's, Ireland's and Venezuela's, which are actually named the *Central Bank*. The *Bank of England* becomes the *bank* on second mention.

The *IMF* may become the *fund* on second mention.

The *World Bank* and the *Fed* (after first spelling it out as the *Federal Reserve*) take initial upper case, although these are shortened, informal names. The *World Bank* becomes the *bank* on second mention.

Treasury bonds issued by America's Treasury should be upper case; *treasury bills* (or *bonds*) of a general kind should be lower case. Avoid *t-bonds* and *t-bills*.

food and drink Lower case should be used for most common or familiar wines, cheeses, grape varieties, for example:

barolo	dim sum	piesporter
bordeaux	emmental	pinotage
brunello	gorgonzola	pont-l'évêque
burgundy	hock	primitivo
champagne	merlot	rioja
chardonnay	moselle	syrah
cheddar	parmesan	zinfandel

But the proper names of particular wines take upper case:
Cheval Blanc Lafite Marqués de Riscal Pontet-Canet

as do some foods and drinks that would look odd lower case:
Bombay duck Nuits St George Parma ham

historical terms

Allies (in the second world war)	the Depression (1930s)
Black Death	Enlightenment
Cultural Revolution	etc (*but* new year)
D-Day	Holocaust (second world war)

Industrial Revolution
Middle Ages
New Deal
Prohibition
Reconstruction

Reformation
Renaissance
Restoration
Thirty Years War
Year of the Dog, Horse, Rat

Note that all other revolutions are lower case, but upper-case for the qualifier: Orange revolution, Green revolution, French revolution.

organisations, institutions, acts, etc

1   Organisations, ministries, departments, institutions, treaties, acts, etc, generally take upper case when their full name (or something pretty close to it, eg, *State Department*) is used.
Amnesty International
Arab League
Bank of England (the bank)
Central Committee
Court of Appeal
the Crown (Britain)
Department for Environment, Food & Rural Affairs (DEFRA)
Department of State (the department)
European Commission
Forestry Commission
Health and Safety at Work Act
High Court
House of Commons
House of Lords
House of Representatives
Household Cavalry
Metropolitan Police
Ministry of Defence
New York Stock Exchange
Oxford University
Politburo
Scottish Parliament (the parliament)
Senate
St Paul's Cathedral (the cathedral)

Supreme Court
Treasury
Treaty of Rome
Welsh Assembly (the assembly)
World Bank (the bank)

2 Organisations with unusual or misleading names, such as the *African National Congress* and *Civic Forum*, may become the *Congress* and the *Forum* on second and subsequent mentions.

3 But most other organisations – agencies, banks, commissions (including the *European Commission* and the *European Union*), etc – take lower case when referred to incompletely on second mention.

4 Informal names
Organisations, committees, commissions, special groups, etc, that are impermanent, ad hoc, local or relatively insignificant should be lower case:
international economic subcommittee of the Senate Foreign Relations Committee;
Market Blandings rural district council;
Oxford University bowls club;
subcommittee on journalists' rights of the National Executive Committee of the Labour Party.

5 Rough descriptions or translations
Use lower case for rough descriptions (*the safety act*, the *American health department*, the *French parliament*, as distinct from its *National Assembly*). If you are not sure whether the English translation of a foreign name is exact or not, assume it is rough and use lower case.

6 Congress and Parliament
Congress and *Parliament* are upper case, unless parliament is used not to describe the institution but the period of time for which it sits:
This bill will not be brought forward until the next parliament.
But *congressional* and *parliamentary* are lower case, as is the *opposition*, even when used in the sense of *her majesty's loyal opposition*.

The *government*, the *administration* and the *cabinet* are always lower case.

After first mention, the *House of Commons* (or *Lords*, or *Representatives*) becomes the *House*.

7 Acts
In America acts given the names of their sponsors (eg, *Glass–Steagall*, *Helms–Burton*) are always rough descriptions (*see above*) and so take a lower-case *act*.

people

1 Ranks and titles
Use upper case when written in conjunction with a name, but lower case when on their own:
Colonel Qaddafi, *but* the colonel
Pope Benedict, *but* the pope
President Obama, *but* the president
Queen Elizabeth, *but* the queen
Vice-President Ansari, *but* the vice-president

Do not write Prime Minister Brown or Defence Secretary Cannon; they are the prime minister, Mr Brown, and the defence secretary, Mr Cannon. You might, however, write Chancellor Merkel.

2 Office-holders
When referred to merely by their office, not by their name, office-holders are lower case:
the chairman of Marks & Spencer
the chancellor of the exchequer
the foreign secretary
the president of the United States
the prime minister
the treasury secretary

The only exceptions are a few titles that would look unduly peculiar without capitals:
Black Rod
Chancellor of the Duchy of Lancaster

Lord Chancellor
Lord Privy Seal
Master of the Rolls
Speaker (in a parliament)
First Lady

and a few exalted people, such as:
the Dalai Lama, the Aga Khan. Also God and the Prophet.

3 Some titles serve as names, and therefore have initial
capitals, though they also serve as descriptions: *the
Archbishop of Canterbury, the Emir of Kuwait.* If you want to
describe the office rather than the individual, use lower case:
*The next archbishop of Canterbury will be a woman. Since the
demise of the ninth duke, there has never been another duke of
Portland.*

places Use upper case for definite geographical places, regions,
areas and countries (*The Hague, Transylvania, Germany*), and
for vague but recognised political or geographical areas (but *see*
Europe above):
Central, South and South-East Asia
East Asia (which is to be preferred to the Far East)
the Gulf
Highlands (of Scotland)
Middle East
Midlands (of England)
North Atlantic
North, Central and South America
South Atlantic
the West (as in the decline of the West), Western
West Country

Use capitals for particular buildings even if the name is not
strictly accurate, eg, the *Foreign Office.*

And if in doubt use lower case (*the sunbelt*).

The *third world* (an unsatisfactory term now that the communist
second world has disappeared) is lower case.

Avoid the *western hemisphere.* Unlike the *southern hemisphere* and the *northern hemisphere*, it is not clear where the *western hemisphere* begins or ends. The *Americas* will usually serve instead.

political terms

1   The full name of political parties is upper case, including the word party:
Communist (if a particular party)
Labour Party
Peasants' Party
Republican Party
Tea Party (though not strictly a party, it looks too odd in lower case)

2   But note that some parties do not have party as part of their names, so this should therefore be lower case:
Greece's New Democracy *party*
India's Congress *party*
Indonesia's Golkar *party*
Turkey's Justice and Development *party*

3   Note that usually only people are:
Democrats   Liberal Democrats
Christian Democrats   Social Democrats

Their parties, policies, candidates, committees, etc, are:
Democratic   Liberal Democratic
Christian Democratic   Social Democratic

But a committee may be Democrat-controlled.

The exceptions are Britain's *Liberal Democrat Party* and Thailand's *Democrat Party*.

4   When referring to a specific party, write *Labour*, the *Republican nominee*, a prominent *Liberal*, etc, but use lower case in looser references to *liberals, conservatism, communists,* etc. *Tories,* however, are upper case, as is *New Labour.*

proper names When forming nouns, adjectives and verbs from proper names, retain the initial capital:
Buddhism   Christian

Finlandisation	Luddite
Gaullism	Maronite
Hindu	Marxist
Hobbesian	Napoleonic
Islamic	Paisleyite
Jacobite	Russify
Leninist	Thatcherism

Exceptions are: *platonic, pyrrhic, draconian.*

Indian castes are upper case and roman. Eg Brahmin, Dalit.
Gypsy should also be upper case.

province, county, river, state are lower case when not strictly
part of the name:

Cabanas province	New York state
Limpopo river	Washington state

Exceptions are: Mississippi River, River Thames, Red River (USA),
Yellow River (China).

trade names Use capitals:
BlackBerry Google Hoover Teflon Valium Jeep

miscellaneous (lower case)

19th amendment (but Article 19)
aborigines
amazon (female warrior)
angst
blacks (and whites)
cabinet
civil servant
civil service
civil war (even America's)
cold war
common market
communist (generally)
constitution (even America's)
cruise missile
first world war
french windows
general synod
gentile
government
Gulf war
Internet
junior (as in George Bush junior)
Kyoto protocol
the left
mafia (any old group of criminals)
miscellaneous (upper case)

mecca (when used loosely, as a mecca for tourists)
new year (but New Year's Day)
Olympic games (and Asian, Commonwealth, European)
opposition
philistine
the pope
the press
the queen
quisling
realpolitik

republican
revolution (everyone's)
the right
second world war
senior (as in George Bush senior)
six-day war
state-of-the-union message
titanic (not the ship)
white paper
wild west
world wide web
young turk

miscellaneous (upper case)

Anglophone (*but* prefer (English-speaking)
Antichrist
anti-Semitism
Atlanticist
the Bar
the Bible
Catholics
CD-ROM
Christ
Christmas Day
Christmas Eve
Coloureds (in South Africa)
the Cup Final
the Davis Cup
Earth (when, and only when, it is being discussed as a planet like Mars or Venus)
Empire (everyone's)
Founding Fathers
Francophone
General Assembly (UN)
Hispanics

Koran
Labour Day
Mafia (the genuine article)
May Day
Mecca (in Saudi Arabia, California and Liberia)
Memorial Day
Moon (when it is Earth's)
New Year's Eve
Pershing missile (because it is named after somebody)
Protestants
the Queen's Speech
Semitic (-ism)
Social Security (in American contexts only, where it is used to mean pensions; what is usually understood by social security elsewhere is welfare in the United States)
Stealth fighter, bomber
Teamster

31

Ten Commandments
Test Match

Tube (London Underground)
Utopia (-n)

See also **abbreviations.**

captions *see* **headings and captions.**

cartel A *cartel* is a group that restricts supply in order to drive up prices. Do not use it to describe any old syndicate or association of producers – especially of drugs.

case "There is perhaps no single word so freely resorted to as a trouble-saver," says Gowers, "and consequently responsible for so much flabby writing." Often you can do without it. *There are many cases of it being unnecessary* is better as *It is often unnecessary. If it is the case that* simply means *If. It is not the case* means *It is not so.*

Cassandra Do not use *Cassandra* just as a synonym for a prophet of doom. The most notable characteristic about her was that her predictions were always correct but never believed.

catalyst A *catalyst* is something that speeds up a chemical reaction while itself remaining unchanged. Do not confuse it with one of the agents.

Central Asian names *see* **names.**

centred on not *around* or *in.*

challenge Although duels and gauntlets have largely disappeared into history, modern life seems to consist of little else but *challenges.* At every turn, every president, every minister, every government, every business, everyone everywhere is faced with *challenges.* No one nowadays has to face a *change, difficulty, task* or *job.* Rather these are *challenges* – fiscal challenges, organisational challenges, structural challenges, regional challenges, demographic challenges, etc. Next time you grab the word *challenge,* drop it at once and think again.

charge If you *charge* intransitively, do so as a bull, cavalry officer or some such, not as an *accuser* (so avoid *The standard of writing was abysmal, he charged*).

charts and tables should, ideally, be understandable without reading the accompanying text. The main point of the heading should therefore be to assist understanding, though if it does so amusingly, so much the better. If the subject of the chart (or table) is unambiguous (because, say, it is in the middle of a story about Germany), the title need not reflect the subject. In that case, however, the subtitle should clearly state: *Number of occasions on which the word Angst appears in German company reports, 2005–10.*

cherry-pick If you must use this cliché, note that *to cherry-pick* means *to engage in careful rather than indiscriminate selection*, whereas *a cherry-picker is a machine for raising pickers (and cleaners and so on) off the ground.*

Chinese is a language. It may be either *Mandarin* or *Cantonese*.

Chinese names *see* **names.**

circumstances stand around a thing, so it is *in*, not *under*, them.

civil society pops up a lot these days, often in the company of *citizenship skills, community leaders, good governance,* the *international community, social capital* and the like ("Development of civil society is social-reality specific" is a typical example). That should serve as a warning. It can, however, be a useful, albeit ill-defined term to describe collectively all non-commercial organisations in between the family and the state. But do not use it as a euphemism for NGOs (non-governmental organisations), which is how it is usually employed.

clerical titles *see* **titles.**

clichés weren't always clichéd. The first person to use *window of opportunity* or *level playing-field* or *accident waiting to happen* was justly pleased with himself. Each is a strong, vivid expression – or was. The trouble is that such expressions have been copied so often that they have lost their vividness. Mass printing made constant repetition easy, which explains how the word cliché came into being: it is the French term for a *stereotype printing plate*. Careful writers since Flaubert, who was so obsessive in his search for freshness that he insisted on anything approaching a cliché being printed in italics, have tried to avoid hackneyed phrases.

In "A Dictionary of Clichés" (1940), Eric Partridge wrote: "Clichés range from fly-blown phrases (*much of a muchness; to all intents and purposes*), metaphors that are now pointless (*lock, stock and barrel*), formulas that have become mere counters (*far be it from me to ...*) – through sobriquets that have lost all their freshness and most of their significance (*the Iron Duke*) – to quotations that are nauseating (*cups that cheer but not inebriate*), and foreign phrases that are tags (*longo intervallo, bête noire*)."

In truth, many of yesterday's clichés have become so much a part of the language that they pass unnoticed; they are like Orwell's dead metaphors. The ones most to be avoided are the latest, the trendiest. Since they usually appeal to people who do not have the energy to pick their own words, they are often found in the wooden prose of bureaucrats, academics and businessmen, though journalese is far from immune.

Clichés numb, rather than stimulate, the reader's brain. Many of the clichés in *The Economist* are phrases like *bite the bullet, confirmed bachelor, eye-watering sums, grinding to a halt, high-profile, honeymoon period, incurable optimist, road maps, tax packages, too close to call, toxic debt, whopping bills.* They serve merely to bore. Far worse are some of those placed in its pages by its managers, which probably induce terminal despair. The following appeared in an advertisement in May 2009: *world-class analysis, key industries, proven track record, strategic, transformative thinking, decisive goal-driven leader, consummate collaborator within a team framework, impactful programmes, strategic and consultative approach, professional in all internal and external interactions, results-driven, relationship-building and communication skills.*

Many of these expressions are meaningless. All are ugly. All are borrowed unthinkingly from the language of other advertisers, and since they appear so often they fail to make an impact. Bureaucrats are inveterate offenders. They delight in posts like *service improvement managers for lifelong disabilities service, heads of offending services* and *human-resources officers.* Their work is always *challenging, exciting, key, strategic* and often *multi-disciplinary.* They are inevitably *committed, creative, dynamic, innovative* and *proactive.* Here is part of a letter from a large London think-tank, explaining that it might be slow in updating members' details because it was improving its computer system. This simple message was conveyed in 125 words, of which these are some:

> The organisation is upgrading its IT infrastructure by introducing a new database which will enable us to store and share information more effectively internally. We embarked upon this major project when it became clear that the current system no longer adequately supported our requirements. When the new system is fully implemented in the autumn it will enable us to more effectively manage our relationship with members and other stakeholders ... We kindly ask for your patience while we resolve any issues over the next two weeks.

Language such as this is so common that its authors have stopped asking themselves whether it means anything, whether the message might make more impact if it were expressed in 20 words rather than 125 or whether anyone will even bother to read it.

Do not add to such tosh. Be especially careful not to borrow the empty phrases of politicians who constantly invoke *paradigm shifts, wake-up calls, supply-side solutions, blue-sky thinking* and *social inclusion,* while asserting their desire to *go the extra mile, push the envelope* and *kick-start the economy. Making a difference* is one of the most fatuous favourites. Thus a former director of communications for the Labour Party could assert that the prime minister, Gordon Brown, was being criticised only because he wanted *to make a difference,* as though the same plea could not have been made for A. Hitler or J. Stalin.

Not all clichés, however, are used unthinkingly. Politicians often resort to hackneyed language to give the impression that they are saying something when they are doing their best to avoid it.

Treat all such stuff as a caution. ("Political language is designed to ... give an appearance of solidity to pure wind." George Orwell)

Nothing betrays the lazy writer faster than fly-blown phrases used in the belief that they are snappy, trendy or cool. Some of these clichés are deliberately chosen, usually from a film or television, or perhaps a politician. Others come into use less wittingly, often from social scientists. If you find yourself using any of the following vogue words, you should stop and ask yourself whether it is the best word for the job, would you have used it in the same context five or ten years ago, and if not why not:

> *address* meaning *answer, deal with, attend to, look at*
> Brits
> *care for* and all caring expressions – how about *look after?*
> *commit to* meaning *commit yourself to*
> *famously:* usually redundant, nearly always irritating
> *focus:* all the world's a stage, not a lens
> *historic:* let historians, not contemporary commentators, be the judge
> *individual:* fine as an adjective and occasionally as a noun, but increasingly favoured by the wooden-tongued as a longer synonym for *man, woman* or *person*
> *inform,* when used as a pretentious alternative to *influence*
> *metrosexual*
> *overseas* – inexplicably, and often wrongly, used to mean *abroad* or *foreign*
> *participate in* – use *take part in,* with more words but fewer syllables
> *process* – a word properly applied to *attempts to bring about*

peace, because they are meant to be evolutionary, but now
often used in place of *talks*
relationship – *relations* can nearly always do the job
resources, especially *human resources*, which may be
personnel, staff or just *people*
supportive – *helpful?*
target – if you are tempted to *target your efforts*, try to *direct*
them instead
transparency – *openness?*
wannabes

Such words should not be banned, but if you find yourself using
them only because you hear others using them, not because
they are the most appropriate ones in the context, you should
avoid them. Overused words and off-the-shelf expressions make
for stale prose.

See also **euphemisms, horrible words, journalese and slang.**

co- This prefix is sometimes useful but now overdone. In the
sentences *He co-founded the company with Sir Alan* or *He co-wrote
"The Left Nation" with Adrian Windback*, the *co-* is unnecessary.
Co-author and *co-sleep* are worse than that. "We want parents
… not to co-sleep with their baby," said Professor Peter Fleming.
This was because "the majority of the co-sleeping deaths
occurred in a hazardous sleeping environment." (*The Times*,
October 14th 2009.)

coiffed not *coiffured*.

collapse (verb) is not transitive. You may *collapse*, but you may not
collapse something.

colons *see* **punctuation.**

come up with Try *suggest, originate* or *produce*.

commas *see* **punctuation.**

commit Do not *commit to*, but by all means *commit yourself to*
something.

community is a useful word in the context of religious or
ethnic groups. But in many others it jars. Not only is it often
unnecessary, it also purports to convey a sense of togetherness
that may well not exist:
The *black community* means *blacks* (or *African-Americans*, etc).
The *business community* means *businessmen* (who are supposed
to be competing, not colluding).
The *homosexual community* means *homosexuals* or *gays*.
The *intelligence community* means *spies*.
The *online community* means *geeks and nerds*.
The *migration and development communities* means *NGOs*.
The *international community*, if it means anything, means *other
countries, aid agencies* or, just occasionally, *the family of nations*.
What the *global community* (*Financial Times*, July 12th 2005)
means is a mystery.

company names Call companies by the names they call themselves.
Here is a selection of names that are sometimes spelt incorrectly.
Economist usage is now to ignore all rogue exclamation marks,
backward letters, etc in company names.

ABN AMRO
Accenture
ACNeilsen
Allied Domecq
Amazon (not Amazon.com)
Anheuser-Busch
AOL
Arthur Andersen
AstraZeneca
AT&T (American Telephone
and Telegraph)
AXA (French Insurance
company)
BAE Systems
Benetton
Berkshire Hathaway
Bertelsmann

BHP Billiton (Australian
mining group)
BlackBerry
Bloomingdale's
BNP Paribas
BP (which no longer refers to
itself as British Petroleum)
BSkyB
BT (British Telecom)
Cadbury Schweppes
Citigroup (Citibank in some
countries)
Coca-Cola
ConocoPhillips
Crédit Agricole
Credit Suisse
DaimlerChrysler

Deloitte Touche Tohmatsu
DuPont
E.On (German utility
  company)
easyJet (but EasyJet at start of
  sentence)
eBay
Eli Lilly
Ericcson (Swedish telecoms
  company)
Exxon Mobil
GlaxoSmithKline
HarperCollins
Hewlett-Packard (HP)
JPMorgan (investment
  banking arm of JP Morgan
  Chase)
J. Sainsbury (Sainsbury's is
  the name above the shop)
Lonrho
L'Oreal
Marks & Spencer
Merrill Lynch
Moody's, rating agency
NASDAQ
News Corporation (News
Corp)
Nielsen/NetRatings
PeopleSoft
PepsiCo
Pfizer
Philip Morris
Philips (Dutch electronics
  multinational)
Pillsbury
PricewaterhouseCoopers
  (abbreviate to pwc)
Procter & Gamble
QinetiQ
Rolls-Royce
Saatchi & Saatchi
Sears, Roebuck
Standard & Poor's
ThyssenKrupp
Toys "R" Us
Vivendi Universal
Vodafone Group
Wal-Mart
WH Smith
Xstrata
Yahoo
ZenithOptimedia

comparatives Take care. One thing may be *many times more
  expensive* than another. It cannot be *many times cheaper*. Indeed,
  it can be cheaper only by a proportion that is less than one. A
  different but similar mistake is to say that *people grew twice as
  poor during a given period*. Instead, say *people's incomes fell by
  half during that period* (if that is what you mean, which, since it
  confuses income with wealth, it may not be).

compare A is compared *with* B when you draw attention to the
  difference. A is compared *to* B only when you want to stress
  their similarity.
  Shall I compare thee to a summer's day?

compound (verb) does not mean *make worse*. It may mean *combine* or, intransitively, it may mean to *agree* or *come to terms*. To *compound a felony* means to *agree for a consideration not to prosecute*. (It is also used, with different senses, as a noun and adjective.)

comprise means *is composed of*. NATO's *force in Afghanistan comprises troops from 42 countries. America's troops make up (not comprise) nearly half the force.* Alternatively, *Nearly half NATO's force in Afghanistan is composed of American troops.*

contemporary *see* **current.**

continuous describes something uninterrupted. *Continual* admits of a break. If your neighbours play loud music every night, it is a *continual* nuisance; it is not a *continuous* one unless the music is never turned off.

contract *see* **subcontract.**

contrast, by or **in** Use *by contrast* only when you are comparing one thing with another: *Somalia is a poor country. By contrast, Egypt is rich.* This means Egypt is rich by comparison with Somalia, though by other standards it is poor. If you are simply noting a difference, say *in contrast: The Joneses spend their holidays in the south of France. In contrast, the Smiths go to south Wales.*

convince should be followed by a noun or, in the passive, *that* or *of*. Do not *convince* people *to* do something. If you want to write *to*, the verb you need is *persuade*. *The prime minister was persuaded to call a June election; he was convinced of the wisdom of doing so only after he had won.*

coruscate means *sparkle* or *throw off flashes of light*, not *wither*, *devastate* or *reduce to wrinkles* (that's *corrugate*).

could is sometimes useful as a variant of *may* or *might: His coalition could (or might) collapse.* But take care. Does *He could call an* *election in June* mean *He might call an election in June* or *He would be allowed to call an election in June?*

council, counsel A *council* is a *body of people*, elected or appointed, that advises, administers, organises, legislates, etc. *Counsel* (noun) means *advice* or *consultation*, or *lawyers who give legal advice and fight cases in court.*

crescendo Not an acme, apogee, peak, summit or zenith but a *passage of increasing loudness.* You cannot therefore *build to a crescendo.*

crisis A *decisive event* or *turning-point.* Many of the economic and political troubles wrongly described as *crises* are really *persistent difficulties, sagas* or *affairs.*

critique is a noun. If you want a verb, try *criticise.*

currencies Use $ as the standard currency and, on first mention of sums in all other currencies, give a dollar conversion in brackets.
   Apart from those currencies that are written out in full (*see below*), write the abbreviation followed by the number. Currencies are not set in small capitals unless they occur as words in text without figures attached: "*Out went the D-mark, in came the euro.*"

Britain
pound, abbreviated as £
pence, abbreviated as p
1p, 2p, 3p, etc to 99p (*not* £0.99)
£6 (*not* £6.00), £6.47
£5,000-6,000 (*not* £5,000-£6,000)
£5m-6m (*not* £5m-£6m)
£5 billion-6 billion (*not* £5-6 billion), £5.2 billion-6.2 billion

America
dollar, abbreviated as $, will do generally; US$ if there is a mixture of dollar currencies (*see below*)
cents, spell out, unless part of a larger number: $4.99

other dollar currencies

A$	Australian dollars	NT$	Taiwanese dollars
C$	Canadian dollars	NZ$	New Zealand dollars
HK$	Hong Kong dollars	S$	Singaporean dollars
M$	Malaysian dollars	Z$	Zimbabwean dollars

Europe

euro, plural euros, abbreviated as €, for those countries that have adopted it.

cents, spell out, unless part of a larger number.

€10 (*not* 10 euros), €10.75

DM, BFr, drachmas, FFr, Italian lire, IR£ (punts), markkas, Asch, Ptas and other currencies of the euro area have all been replaced by €, but may turn up in historical references.

DKr Danish krone (plural kroner)

IKr Icelandic krona (plural kronur)

NKr Norwegian krone (plural kroner)

SFr Swiss franc, SFr1m (*not* 1m Swiss francs)

SKr Swedish krona (plural kronor)

sums in all other currencies are written in full, with the number first.

Brazil, real, 100m reais

China, yuan, 100m yuan (*not* renminbi) (*see below*)

India, rupee, 100m rupees

Nigeria, naira, 100m naira

peso currencies, 100m pesos

South Africa, rand, 100m rand (*not* rands)

Turkey, Turkish lira, 100m liras

But Japan, yen ¥, ¥1,000 (*not* 1,000 yen)

China Properly, Chinese sums are expressed as, eg, 1 yuan rmb, meaning 1 yuan renminbi. *Yuan*, which means *money*, is the Chinese unit of currency. *Renminbi*, which means the *people's currency*, is the description of the yuan, as sterling is the description of the pound. Use *yuan*.

See also **figures**; and **currencies and measures** in Part 3.

current, contemporary *Current* and *contemporary* mean *at that time,* not necessarily *at this time.* So a series of current prices from 1960 to 1970 will not be in *today's prices,* just as *contemporary art* in 1800 was not *modern art. Contemporary history* is a contradiction in terms.

cusp is a *pointed end* or a *horn* of, for example, the Moon, or *the point at which two branches of a curve meet.* So it is odd to write, say, "Japan is on the cusp of a recovery" unless you think that recovery is about to end.

cyber-expressions Most cyber-terms are hyphenated: *cyber-attack, cyber-soccer,* etc, but *cybercrime, cybernetics, cyberspace* and *cyberwars.*

dashes *see* **punctuation.**

data It cannot be emphasised enough that this is a plural (singular, *datum*), despite its almost universal use as a singular noun. Do not be cowed by the majority.

dates month, day, year, in that order, with no commas:

July 5th	1996–99
Monday July 5th	2005–10
July 5th 2009	1998–2009
July 27th–August 3rd 2010	1990s
July 2002	

Do not write *on June 10th–14th*; prefer *between June 10th and 14th*. If, say, ministers are to meet over two days, write *on December 14th and 15th*.

Do not burden the reader with dates of no significance, but give a date rather than just *last week*, which can cause confusion. *This week* and *next week* are permissible.

Dates are often crucial to an account of events, but sentences (and, even more, articles) that begin with a date can be clumsy and off-putting. *This week Congress is due to consider the matter* is often better put as *Congress is due to consider the matter this week*. The effect is even more numbing if a comma is inserted: *This week, Congress is due to consider the matter*, though this construction is sometimes merited when emphasis is needed on the date.

Dates that require AD or BC should be set as one unhyphenated word (76AD, 55BC), with the letters in small capitals after the number. The same applies to CE (common era) and BCE (before common era), though neither must be used in *The Economist*.

deal (verb) Transitively, *deal* means distribute: "He was dealt two aces, two kings and a six." Intransitively, *deal* means *engage in business*. Do not *deal* drugs, horses, weapons, etc; *deal in* them.

decimate means to destroy a proportion (originally a tenth) of a group of people or things, not to destroy them all or nearly all.

demographics used not to be a word at all, but has become a useful term for *facts about births and deaths*, and *the size and distribution of population*, and it would be foolish to ban it.

deprecate, depreciate To *deprecate* is to *argue* or *plead against* (by prayer or otherwise). To *depreciate* is to *lower in value*.

different from not *to* or *than*.

dilemma Not just any old awkwardness but one with horns, being, properly, a form of argument (the horned syllogism) in which you find yourself committed to accept one of two propositions each of which contradicts your original contention. Thus a *dilemma* offers the choice between two alternatives, each with equally nasty consequences.

discreet, discrete *Discreet* means *circumspect* or *prudent*. *Discrete* means *separate* or *distinct*. Remember that "Questions are never indiscreet. Answers sometimes are." (Oscar Wilde)

disinterested means *impartial*; *uninterested* means *bored*. "Disinterested curiosity is the lifeblood of civilisation." (G.M. Trevelyan)

Dominicans Take care. Do they come from Dominica? Or the Dominican Republic? Or are they friars?

douse, dowse *Douse* means to *throw water over something* or *extinguish a light or a fire. Dowse* means to *search for underground water with a divining rod.*

down to *down to earth* yes, but "Occasional court victories are not down to human rights." (*The Economist*) No: *down to* does not mean *attributable to, the responsibility of* or even *up to* (*It's up to you*). Use *caused by* or *the result of.*

due process is a technical term, or piece of jargon, which was first used in England in 1355. It comes in two forms, *substantive due process*, which relates to the duties of governments to act rationally and proportionally when doing anything that affects citizens' rights, and *procedural due process*, which relates to the need for fair procedures. If you use the expression, make sure it is clear what you mean by it.

due to when used to mean *caused by* must follow a noun, as in *The cancellation, due to rain, of ...* Do not write *It was cancelled due to rain.* If you mean *because of* and for some reason are reluctant to say it, you probably want *owing to. It was cancelled owing to rain* is all right.

Dutch names *see* **names.**

earnings Do not write *earnings* when you mean *profits* (try to say if they are *operating, gross, pre-tax* or *net*).

-ee *employees, evacuees, detainees, divorcee, referees, refugees* but, please, no *attendees* (those attending), *draftees* (conscripts), *enrollees* (participants), *escapees* (escapers), *indictees* (the indicted), *retirees* (the retired), or *standees*. A *divorcee* may be male or female.

e-expressions Except at the start of a sentence, the *e-* is lower case and hyphenated:

e-book   e-commerce
e-business   e-mail

Computer terms are also usually lower case:
dotcom
home-page
laptop
online
the net (and internet)
the web, website and world wide web

but Wi-Fi

When giving *websites*, do not include *http://*. Just *www* is enough: *www.economist.com*. But it should be included for websites that do not use *www*, eg *http://twitter.com*.

See also **cyber-expressions**.

effect the verb, means to *accomplish*, so *The novel effected a change in his attitude. See also* **affect**.

-effective, -efficient *Cost-effective* sounds authoritative, but does it mean *good value for money, gives a big bang for the buck* or just plain *cheap*? If *cheap*, say *cheap*. *Energy-efficient* is also dubious. Does it mean *thrifty, economical* or something else? *Efficiency* is the *ratio of energy put out to energy put in.*

effectively, in effect *Effectively* means *with effect*; if you mean *in effect*, say it. *The matter was effectively dealt with on Friday* means it was *done well* on Friday. *The matter was, in effect, dealt with on Friday* means it was *more or less attended to* on Friday.

either ... or *see* **none.**

elections *see* **grammar and syntax.**

elite, elitist Once a neutral word meaning a *chosen group* or *the pick of the bunch*, *elite* is now almost always used pejoratively. *Elitist* and *elitism* are even more reprehensible. No matter that the words have their roots in the French verb *élire*, to elect, and the Latin *eligere*, to pick out; if you believe in government by a chosen group, or are a member of such a group, you are a reprobate. Only *elite forces* seem to escape censure. Though scornful of elites in education and politics, most people, when taken hostage, are happy to be rescued by elite troops. Use these words with care.

enclave, exclave An *enclave* is a piece of territory or territorial water entirely surrounded by foreign territory (Andorra, Ceuta, Kaliningrad, Melilla, Nagorno-Karabakh, Nakhichevan, San Marino). An *exclave* is the same thing, viewed differently, if, and only if, it belongs to another country.

endemic, epidemic *Endemic* means *prevalent* or *generally found in a place or population*. *Epidemic* means *prevalent among a population at a particular time.*

enormity means a *crime, sin* or *monstrous wickedness*. It does not mean *immensity.*

environment is often unavoidable, but it's not a pretty word. Avoid *the business environment, the school environment, the work environment,* etc. Try to rephrase the sentence – *conditions for business, at school, at work,* etc. *Surroundings* can sometimes do the job. In a *writing environment* you may want to make use of your correction fluid, rubber (or American eraser) or delete key.

epicentre means *that point on the surface* (usually the Earth's) *above the centre of something below* (usually an earthquake). So Mr Putin was not at the *epicentre* of the dispute, he was at its *centre*.

The *hypocentre*, in contrast, is *the place on the surface* (usually of the earth) *below something above* (usually an explosion). It is the same as *ground zero*. At Hiroshima in 1945, it was 580 metres above the ground.

eponymous is the adjective of *eponym*, which is *the person or thing after which something is named.* So George Canning was the *eponymous hero* of the Canning Club, Hellen was the *eponymous ancestor* of the Hellenes (Greeks), Ninus was the *eponymous founder* of Nineveh. Do not say *John Sainsbury, the founder of the eponymous supermarket.* Rather he was the *eponymous founder of J. Sainsbury's.* The word is ugly, though, and usually unnecessary.

ethnic groups Your first concern should be to avoid giving offence. But also avoid mealy-mouthed **euphemisms** and terms that have not generally caught on despite promotion by pressure-groups. *Ethnic* meaning *concerning nations or races*, or even something ill-defined in between, is a useful word. But do not be shy of *race* and *racial*. After several years in which *race* was seen as a purely social concept, not a scientific one, the term is coming back among scientists as a shorthand way of speaking about genetic rather than cultural or political differences. *See also* **political correctness.**

Africans may be descended from Asians, Europeans or black Africans. If you specifically mean the last, write *black Africans*, not simply *Africans*.

Anglo-Saxon is not a synonym for *English-speaking*. Neither the United States nor Australia is an Anglo-Saxon country; nor is Britain. Anglo-Saxon capitalism does not exist.

Asians In Britain, but nowhere else, *Asians* is often used to mean *immigrants and their descendants from the Indian subcontinent*. Many such people are coming to dislike the term, and many foreigners must assume it means people from all over Asia, so take care. Note that, even in the usage peculiar to Britain, *Asian* is not synonymous with *Muslim*.

blacks In many countries, including the United States, many black people are happy to be called *blacks*, although some prefer to be *African-Americans*. *Black* is shorter and more straightforward, but use either. Use *Native American* for indigenous Americans, to avoid confusion with the growing number of Indian-Americans.

mixed race Do not call people who are neither pure white nor pure black *browns*. People of mixed race in South Africa are *Coloureds*. Note the capital.

other groups The inhabitants of *Azerbaijan* are *Azerbaijanis*, some of whom, but not all, are *Azeris*. Those *Azeris* who live in other places, such as Iran, are not *Azerbaijanis*. Similarly, many Croats are not Croatian, many Serbs not Serbian, many Uzbeks not Uzbekistanis, etc.

Spanish-speakers in the United States When writing about Spanish-speaking people in the United States, use either *Latino* or *Hispanic* as a general term, but try to be specific (eg, Mexican-American). Many Latin Americans (eg, those from Brazil) are not Hispanic.

euphemisms Avoid, where possible, euphemisms and circumlocutions, especially those promoted by interest-groups keen to please their clients or organisations anxious to avoid embarrassment. This does not mean that good writers should be insensitive to giving offence: on the contrary, if you are to

be persuasive, you would do well to be courteous. But a good
writer owes something to plain speech, the English language
and the truth, as well as to manners. **Political correctness** can be
carried too far.

So, in most contexts, *offending* behaviour is probably
criminal behaviour. *Female teenagers* are *girls*, not *women*. *Living
with mobility impairment* probably means *wheelchair-bound*.
Developing countries are often *stagnating* or even *regressing* (try
poor) countries. The *underprivileged* may be *disadvantaged*, but
are more likely just *poor* (the very concept of *underprivilege* is
absurd, since it implies that some people receive less than their
fair share of something that is by definition an advantage or
prerogative).

Remember that euphemisms are the stock-in-trade of people
trying to obscure the truth. Thus Enron's *document-management
policy* simply meant *shredding*. France's proposed *solidarity
contribution* on airline tickets was a *tax*. Bankers' *guaranteed
bonuses* are *salaries* (or fractions thereof).

Take particular care if you borrow the language of politicians,
especially when they are trying to justify a war. "They make
a wilderness and call it peace," wrote Tacitus nearly 2,000
years ago, quoting Calgalus, a British chief whose people had
suffered at the hands of the Romans. Orwell was equally acute
in pointing out decades ago how terms like *transfer of population*
and *rectification of frontiers* put names on things without calling
up mental pictures of them. *Friendly fire, body count, prisoner
abuse, smart bombs, surgical strike, collateral damage* have been
coined more recently with the same ends in mind. The Reagan
administration spoke of its airborne invasion of Grenada in
1983 as a *vertical insertion*. The butchers of the Balkans produced
ethnic cleansing, and the jihadists of al-Qaeda have offered
sacred explosions in place of Islamically incorrect *suicide bombs*.
The Bush administration, with its all-justifying *war on terror*
(prosecuted with the help of the *Patriot Act*), provided more
than its fair share of bland misnomers. Its practice of *enhanced
interrogation* was *torture*, just as its practice of *extraordinary
rendition* was probably *torture contracted out to foreigners* and
its *self-injurious behaviour incidents* at Guantánamo Bay were

attempted suicides. The president's ensuing *reputational problem* just meant he was *mistrusted.*

Orwell would surely have put *human-rights abuses* in the same category of nerve-deadening understatement as *pacification* and *elimination of unreliable elements.* The term may occasionally be useful, but try to avoid it by rephrasing the sentence more pithily and accurately. *The army is accused of committing numerous human-rights abuses* probably means *The army is accused of torture and murder. Decommissioning weapons* means *disarming.* A *high-net-worth individual* is a *rich man* or *rich woman. Zero-percent financing* means an *interest-free loan. Quantitative easing* means *increasing the money supply. Non-observable inputs* are *assumptions used in self-serving guesswork. Intimate apparel* is *underwear.*

See also **affirmative action.**

Euro- is the prefix for anything relating to the European Union; *euro-* is the prefix for anything relating to the currency. The usual rules apply for the full, proper names (with informal equivalents on the right below). Thus:

European Commission	the commission
European Parliament	the parliament
European Union	the Union
Treaty of Rome	the Rome treaty
Treaty on European Union	the Maastricht treaty
Treaty of Lisbon	the Lisbon treaty

The EU grouping may be called EU-15, EU-27.

When making *Euro-* or *euro-words*, always introduce a hyphen. Exceptions are:
Europhile Europhobe Eurosceptic Eurobond Euroyen bond

Prefer *euro zone* or *euro area* (two words, no hyphen) to *euro-land.*
CAP is the *common agricultural policy.*
EMU stands for *economic and* (not *European*) *monetary union.*
ERM is the *exchange-rate mechanism.*
IGC is an *inter-governmental conference.*

ex- (and former) Be careful. A *Labour Party ex-member* has lost his seat; an *ex-Labour member* has lost his party.

execute means *put to death by law.* Do not use it as a synonym for *murder.* An *extra-judicial execution* is a contradiction in terms. (*See* **assassinate**.)

existential Often used, seldom understood, even it seems by those who use it, *existential* means *of* or *pertaining to existence.* In logic it may mean *predicating existence,* and in other philosophical contexts, *relating to existentialism.* It is sometimes used in such phrases as *existential threat* or *existential crisis,* where the author wants it to mean a threat to the existence (of Israel, say) or a crisis that calls into the question the existence of something (eg, NATO). But in most instances, including most in *The Economist,* it seems to serve no purpose other than to make the writer believe he is impressing his readers.

fact *The fact that* can often be reduced to *that*, but not always. Check whether it confuses the start of a sentence, as it sometimes does.

factoid A *factoid* is something that sounds like a fact, is thought by many to be a fact (perhaps because it is repeated so often), but is not in fact a fact.

fed up *with*, not *of*. Similarly, *bored with*, not *of*.

federalist in Britain, someone who believes in centralising the powers of associated states; in the United States and Europe, someone who believes in decentralising them.

fellow Often unnecessary, especially before *countrymen* ("Friends, Romans, *fellow-countrymen*"?).

feral can mean *brutish* or *uncultivated*, but is best used of plants, animals, children, etc, that were once tamed or domesticated but have *run wild*.

ferment, foment When you *ferment*, what you are doing is to cause something to effervesce, like yeast. But you *foment* trouble, sedition, revolution.

fewer than, less than *Fewer* (not *less*) *than seven speeches, fewer than seven samurai.* Use *fewer*, not *less*, with numbers of individual items or people. *Less than £200, less than 700 tonnes of oil, less than a third*, because these are measured quantities or proportions, not individual items.

fief not *fiefdom*.

figures Never start a sentence with a figure; write the number in words instead.

Use words for simple numerals from one to ten inclusive, except: in references to pages; in percentages (eg, 4%); and in sets of numerals, some of which are higher than ten.
Deaths from this cause in the past three years were 14, 9 and 6.

Always use numbers with units of measurement, even for those less than ten:
4 metres, 9 miles, but *four cows*
3D is in small caps.

It is occasionally permissible to use words rather than numbers when referring to a rough or rhetorical figure (such as *a thousand curses, a hundred years of solitude*).

In all other cases, though, use figures for numerals from 11 upwards.

first to tenth centuries, the 11th century	a 29-year-old man
20th century, 21st century	a man in his 20s
20th-century ideas	20th anniversary
in 100 years' time	40-fold (but fourfold)
two and a half years later	30-something

The *Thirty Years War* is an exception.

decimal point Use figures for all numerals that include a decimal point (eg, 4.25).

fractions Figures may be appropriate for fractions, if the context is either technical or precise, or both:
Though the poll's figures were supposed to be accurate to within 1%, his lead of 4¼ points turned out on election day to be minus 3½.

Where precision is less important but it is nonetheless impossible to shoot off the fraction, words may look better:
Though the beast was sold as a two-year-old, it turned out to be two and a half times that.

Fractions should be hyphenated (one-half, three-quarters, etc)

and, unless they are attached to whole numbers (8½, 29¾), spelled out in words, even when the figures are higher than ten:
He gave a tenth of his salary to the church, a twentieth to his mistress and a thirtieth to his wife.

fractions and decimals Do not compare a fraction with a decimal. So avoid:
The rate fell from 3¼% to 3.1%.

Fractions are more precise than decimals (3.33 neglects an infinity of figures that are embraced by ¹/3), but your readers probably do not think so. You should therefore use fractions for rough figures:
Kenya's population is growing at 3½% a year. A hectare is 2½ acres.
and decimals for more exact ones:
The retail price index is rising at an annual rate of 10.6%.

But treat all numbers with respect. That usually means resisting the precision of more than one decimal place, and generally favouring rounding off. Beware of phoney over-precision.

hyphens and figures Do not use a hyphen in place of *to* except with figures:
He received a sentence of 15–20 years in jail but *He promised to escape within three to four weeks.*

Latin usage It is outdated to use Latin words. So, with figures, do not write *per caput, per capita* or *per annum.* Use:
a head or *per head*
a person or *per person*
a year or *per year*
2 litres of water per person
prices rose by 10% a year

*See also **per caput**.*

measurements In most non-American contexts prefer:
hectares to acres
kilometres (or *km*) to miles
metres to yards
litres to gallons

kilos (*kg*) to lb
tonnes to tons

Celsius to Fahrenheit, etc

1   In American contexts, you may use the measurements more
    familiar to Americans (though remember that American
    pints, quarts, gallons, etc, are smaller than imperial ones).
        Regardless of which you choose, you should give an
    equivalent, on first use, in the other units:
    *It was hoped that after improvements to the engine the car
    would give 20km to the litre (47 miles per American gallon),
    compared with its present average of 15km per litre.*

2   Remember that in only a few countries do you now buy
    petrol in imperial gallons. In America it is sold in American
    gallons; in most other places it is sold in litres.

3   Note that a four-by-four vehicle can be a 4×4.

million, billion, trillion, quadrillion Use *m* for million. Spell out
billion and trillion (though their conventional abbreviations are
bn and *trn*).
8m   8 billion
£8m   €8 billion

A *billion* is a thousand million, a *trillion* a thousand billion, a
quadrillion a thousand trillion.

per cent, percentage points Use the sign % instead of *per cent*.
But write *percentage*, never *%age* (though in most contexts
proportion or *share* is preferable).

A fall from 4% to 2% is a drop of two percentage points, or of
50%, but not of 2%. (*See also* **per cent.**)

ranges Write:
5,000–6,000
5–6%
5m–6m (*not* 5–6m)
5 billion–6 billion

But:

Sales rose from 5m to 6m (not *5m–6m*); *estimates ranged between 5m and 6m* (not *5m–6m*).

ratios Where *to* is being used as part of a ratio, it is usually best to spell it out.

They decided, by nine votes to two, to put the matter to the general assembly, which voted, 27 to 19, to insist that the ratio of vodka to tomato juice in a bloody mary should be at least one to three, though the odds of this being so in most bars were put at no better than 11 to 4.

Where a ratio is being used adjectivally, figures and hyphens may be used, but only if one of the figures is greater than ten:

a 50–20 vote

a 19–9 vote

Otherwise, spell out the figures and use *to*:

a two-to-one vote

a ten-to-one probability

finally Do not use *finally* when you mean *at last. Richard Burton finally marries Liz Taylor* would have been all right second time round but not first.

firm Accountants', consultants', lawyers' and other partnerships are *firms*, not *companies*. Huge enterprises, like GE, GM, Ford, Microsoft and so on, should, by contrast, normally be called *companies*, although such outfits can sometimes be called *firms* for variety.

flaunt, flout *Flaunt* means display; *flout* means disdain. If you *flout* this distinction, you will *flaunt* your ignorance.

focus can be a useful word. It is shorter than *concentrate* and sharper than *look at.* But it is overused.

footnotes, sources, references *see* **footnotes, sources, references** in Part 3.

foreign languages and translation Occasionally, a foreign language may provide the *mot juste*. But try not to use foreign words and phrases unless there is no English alternative, which is unusual.

names of foreign companies, institutions, groups, parties, etc should usually be translated. So:
the Dutch People's Party for Freedom and Democracy (*not* the Volkspartij voor Vrijheid en Democratie
the German Christian Democratic Union (*not* the Christlich Demokratische Union)
the Shining Path (*not* Sendero Luminoso)
the National Assembly (*not* the Assemblée Nationale)

But if an abbreviation is also given, that may be the initials of the foreign name:
UMP for France's Union for a Presidential Majority
SPD for the Social Democratic Party of Germany
PAN for Mexico's National Action Party

Break this rule when the name is better known untranslated:
Forza Italia
Médecins Sans Frontières
Parti Québécois (Canada)
yakuza (*not* 8-9-3)

placenames Some placenames are better translated if they are well known in English:
St Mark's Square in Venice (*not* Piazza San Marco)
the Elysée Palace (*not* the Palais de l'Elysée)

titles of foreign books, films, etc The titles of foreign books, films, plays, operas and TV programmes present difficulties. Some are so well known that they are unlikely to need translation:
"Das Kapital" "Mein Kampf" "Le Petit Prince" "Die Fledermaus"

And sometimes the meaning of the title may be unimportant in the context, so a translation is not necessary:
"Hiroshima, Mon Amour"

But often the title will be significant, and you will want to translate it. One solution, easy with classics, is simply to give the English translation:

"One Hundred Years of Solitude" "The Leopard" "War and Peace" "The Tin Drum"

This is usually the best practice to follow with pamphlets, articles and non-fiction, too.

But sometimes, especially with books and films that are little known among English-speakers or unobtainable in English · (perhaps you are reviewing one), you may want to give both the original title and a translation, thus:

"11 Septembre 2001: l'Effroyable Imposture" ("September 11th 2001: The Appalling Deception")

"La Règle du Jeu" ("The Rules of the Game")

"La Traviata" ("The Sinner")

Foreign titles do not need to be set in italics. Treat them as if they were in English.

Note that book publishers follow different rules here. (*See* **italics**.)

translating words and phrases If you want to translate a foreign word or phrase, even if it is the name of a group or newspaper or party, just put it in brackets without inverted commas, so:

Arbeit macht frei (work makes free)

jihad (struggle)

Pravda (Truth)

zapatero (shoemaker)

forensic means *pertaining to courts of law* (held by the Romans in the forum) or, more loosely, *the application of science to legal issues. Forensic medicine* is *medical jurisprudence. Forensic* does not mean *very careful* or *very detailed.*

forgo, forego *Forgo* means do without; it forgoes the *e. Forego* means go before. A *foregone conclusion* is one that is predetermined; a *forgone conclusion* is non-existent.

former *see* **ex-**.

former and latter Avoid the use of *the former* and *the latter* whenever possible. It usually causes confusion.

Frankenstein was not the monster, but its creator.

free is an adjective or an adverb (and also a transitive verb), so you cannot have or do anything *for free*. Either you have it *free* or you have it *for nothing*.

French names *see* **names.**

fresh is not a synonym for *new* or *more*. "A few hundred fresh bodies are being recovered every day," reported *The Economist* improbably, two months after a tsunami had struck. Use with care.

full stops *see* **punctuation.**

fulsome is an old word that Americans generally use only to mean *cloying, insincere* or *excessively flattering*. In British English it can also mean *copious, abundant* or *lavish*.

fund (verb) is a technical term, meaning to convert floating debt into more or less permanent debt at fixed interest. Try to avoid it if you mean to *finance* or to *pay for*.

garner means *store*, not *gather*.

gearing is an ugly word which, if used, needs to be explained. It may be either the *ratio of debt to equity* or the *ratio of debt to total capital employed*. (*See also* **leverage**.)

gender is nowadays used in several ways. One is common in feminist writing, where the term has a technical meaning. "One is not born a woman, one becomes one," argued Simone de Beauvoir: in other words, one chooses one's gender. In such a context it would be absurd to use the word *sex*; the term must be *gender*. But, in using it thus, try to explain what you mean by it. Even feminists do not agree on a definition.

The primary use of *gender*, though, is in grammar, where it is applied to words, not people. If someone is female, that is her *sex*, not her *gender*. (The gender of *Mädchen*, the German word for girl, is neuter, as is *Weib*, a wife or woman.) So do not use *gender* as a synonym for *sex*. *Gender studies* probably means *feminism*.

gentlemen's agreement not *gentleman's*.

German names *see* **names**.

get is an adaptable verb, but it has its limits. A man does not *get* sacked or promoted, he *is* sacked or promoted. Nor does a prize-winner *get to* shake hands with the president, or spend the money all at once; he *gets the chance to*, is *able to*, or *allowed to*.

global Globalisation can go to the head. It is not necessary to describe, eg, the head of Baker & Mackenzie as the *global head* of that firm. And what is a *global vacancy* (as advertised by The Economist Group)? And avoid saying "now that we're all part of a global world", unless you have hitherto believed the Earth to be flat.

good in parts is what the curate said about an egg that was wholly bad. He was trying to be polite.

gourmet, gourmand *Gourmet* means *epicure*; *gourmand* means *greedy-guts*.

governance *Corporate governance* has now entered the language as a useful, albeit ugly and ill-defined, term to describe the rules relating to the conduct of business. The popularity of *governance* in other contexts is more difficult to understand. An old word, it had largely fallen into suitable disuse until Harold Wilson chose it in 1976 for the title of his memoirs ("The Governance of Britain"), presumably to dignify an undistinguished prime ministership. It means simply *government*, a word that serves the same purpose without any of the pretensions or pomposity of *governance*.

grammar and syntax Take care in the construction of your sentences and paragraphs. A single issue of *The Economist* contained the following:
When closed at night, the fear is that this would shut off rather than open up part of the city centre.
Unlike Canary Wharf, the public will be able to go to the top to look out over the city.
Only a couple of months ago, after an unbroken string of successes in state and local elections, pollsters said …

Some hints are provided here on avoiding pitfalls, infelicities and mistakes; this is not a comprehensive guide to English grammar and syntax.

a or the Strictly, *Barclays* is a *British bank*, not *the British bank*, just as *Toyota* is *a car company*, not *the car company*, and *Angela Gheorghiu* is *an opera singer*, not *the opera singer*. If it seems absurd to describe someone or something thus – that is, with the indefinite article – you can probably dispense with the description altogether or insert an extra word or two that may be useful to the reader: *Toyota, the world's biggest car company in 2009; Mick Jagger of the Rolling Stones.*

active or passive? Be direct. Use the active tense. *A hit B* describes the event more concisely than *B was hit by A.*

adjectives and adverbs Adjectives qualify nouns, adverbs modify verbs. If you have a sentence that contains the words *firstly, secondly, more importantly,* etc, they almost certainly ought to be *first, second, more important.*

adjectives of proper nouns If proper nouns have adjectives, use them.
Crimean war (*not* the Crimea war)
Dutch East India Company (*not* the Holland East India Company)
Lebanese (*not* Lebanon) civil war
Mexican (*not* Mexico) problem
Pakistani (*not* Pakistan) government

It is permissible to use the noun as an adjective if to do otherwise would cause confusion.

An *African initiative* suggests the proposal came *from Africa*, whereas an *Africa initiative* suggests it was *about Africa*.

Californian, Texan Do not feel you have to follow American convention in using words like *Californian* and *Texan* only as nouns. In British English, it is quite acceptable to write a *Californian* (not *California*) *judge*, *Texan* (not *Texas*) *scandal*, etc. "Mr Gedge ... was not fond of St Rocque, and this morning it would have seemed less attractive to him than ever, for three of his letters bore Californian postmarks and their contents had aggravated the fever of his home-sickness." (P.G. Wodehouse, "Hot Water")

collective nouns – singular or plural? There is no firm rule about the number of a verb governed by a singular collective noun. It is best to go by the sense – that is, whether the collective noun stands for a single entity:
The council was elected in March.
The me generation has run its course.
The staff is loyal.

or for its constituents:
The council are at sixes and sevens.
The preceding generation are all dead.
The staff are at each other's throats.
Do not, in any event, slavishly give all singular collective nouns singular verbs: *The couple are now living apart* is preferable to *The couple is now living apart.*

> **majority** When it is used in an abstract sense, it takes the singular; when it is used to denote the elements making up the majority, it should be plural.
> *A two-thirds majority is needed to amend the constitution*
> but *A majority of the Senate were opposed.*
> *A majority of* can often be replaced by *most.*

> **number** Rule: *The number is ...; A number are ...*

> **pair and couple** Treat both a *pair* and a *couple* as plural.

comparisons Take care, too, when making comparisons, to compare like with like:
The Belgian economy is bigger than Russia should be *Belgium's economy is bigger than Russia's.*

An advertisement for *The Economist* declared,
Our style and our whole philosophy are different from other publications. Only changing *publications* to *publications'* could turn this into sense.

contractions Don't overdo the use of *don't, isn't, can't, won't,* etc.

false possessive An 's at the end of a word, in the possessive or genitive case, does the job of *of.* An increasingly common practice, especially among broadcasters and sometimes in *The Economist,* is to use it to do the job of *in.* Thus places or buildings are described as, eg, *New York's Chrysler Building, Edinburgh's Usher Hall* or *Belfast's Shankill Road.* Do not commit this sin. The Chrysler Building is *in* New York, not *of* it, just as Shankill Road is *in* Belfast and the Usher Hall is *in* Edinburgh.

genitive Take care with the genitive. It is fine to say a *friend of Bill's,* just as you would say *a friend of mine,* so you can also say *a friend of Bill's and Carol's.* But it is also fine to say a *friend of Bill,* or *a friend of Bill and Carol.* What you must not say is *Bill and Carol's friend.* If you wish to use that construction, you must say *Bill's and Carol's friend,* which is cumbersome.

gerunds Respect the gerund. Gerunds look like participles – *running, jumping, standing* – but are more noun-like, and should never therefore be preceded by a personal pronoun. So the following are wrong: *I was awoken by him snoring, He could not prevent them drowning, Please forgive me coming late.*

Those sentences should have ended:
his snoring, their drowning, my coming late.

In other words, use the possessive adjective rather than the personal pronoun.

indirect speech If you use indirect speech in the past tense, you must change the tense of the speaker's words appropriately: *Before he died, he said, "I abhor the laziness that is commonplace nowadays"* becomes *Before he died, he said he abhorred the laziness that was commonplace nowadays.*

masculine and feminine Several English nouns have both a masculine and a feminine form, for example:

alumnus, alumna	man, woman
compère, commère	prince, princess
Filipino, Filipina	testator, testatrix
Latino, Latina	widow, widower

nouns acting as verbs Do not force nouns or other parts of speech to act as verbs: *A woman who was severely brain-damaged in 2000* would be better put as *A woman whose brain was severely damaged in 2000* (unless, remarkably, she was no longer brain-damaged at some later date).

participle Do not use a participle unless you make it clear what it applies to. Here are some examples of confused construction:
Proceeding along this line of thought, the cause of the train crash becomes clear.
Looking out from the city's tallest building, the houses stretch for miles and miles.

plural nouns

1 The *-ics* words on page 69 (abstract nouns) are plural when preceded by *the*, or *the* plus an adjective, or with a possessive. For example:
The dynamics of the dynasty were dysfunctional.
The complicated politics of Afghanistan have a logic all their own.
The athletics take place in London.

2 These are plural:

antics	histrionics
atmospherics	hysterics
basics	statistics
graphics	tactics

Specifics are discouraged (try *details*).

3 *Data, elite* (as a group) and *media* are plural. So are *whereabouts* and *headquarters*.

4 *Elections* are not always plural. If, as in the United States, several votes (for the presidency, the Senate, the House of Representatives, etc) are held on the same day, it is correct to talk about *elections*. But in, say, Britain parliamentary polls are usually held on their own, in a single *general election*. *The opposition demanded an election* is often preferable to *The opposition demanded fresh elections*. And to write *The next presidential elections are due in 2015* suggests there will be more than one presidential poll in that year.

5   The *Taliban* are plural. The singular is *Talib*.
Make sure that plural nouns have plural verbs. Too often, in
the pages of *The Economist*, they do not.
Kogalym today is one of the few Siberian oil towns which are
[not is] *almost habitable.*

What better evidence that snobbery and elitism still hold [not
holds] *back ordinary British people?* – and this in a leader on
education.

quoting If you wish to quote someone, either give a date or use
the present tense:
*"He leaves a legacy of wisdom," said John Smith the next day or ...
says Mr John Smith.*

singular nouns

1   A *government*, a *party*, a *company* (whether Tesco or Marks &
Spencer) and a *partnership* (Skidmore, Owings & Merrill) are
all *it* and take a singular verb.

2   *Brokers* are singular.
Legg Mason Wood Walk is preparing a statement.
So avoid:
*stockbrokers Morgan Stanley Smith Barney, bankers JPMorgan
Chase or accountants Ernst & Young.*

3   *Chemical, drug, pension:* prefer the singular when referring to:
chemical (*not* chemicals) companies
drug- (*not* drugs) traffickers
pension (*not* pensions) systems

4   Countries are singular, even if their names look plural.
*The Philippines has a congressional system, as does the United
States; the Netherlands does not.*
The United Nations is also singular.

5   Abstract nouns that look plural when being used generally,
without the definite article, an adjective or a possessive, are
singular. For example:

acoustics	ballistics	economics
athletics	dynamics	kinetics

mathematics	physics	propaganda
mechanics	politics	statics

when being used generally, without the definite article, are singular. For example:

"Economics is the dismal science" (Carlyle).

"Politics is the art of the possible" (Bismarck).

Statics is a branch of physics.

6 Some games are singular:

billiards	darts
bowls	fives

But teams that take the name of a town, country or university are plural, even when they look singular:
England were bowled out for 56.

7 *Law and order* defies the rules of grammar and is singular.

split infinitives Happy the man who has never been told that it is wrong to split an infinitive: the ban is pointless. Unfortunately, to see the rule broken is so annoying to so many people that you should try to observe it, unless it makes the sentence impossibly arch. Changing the sentence construction may help.

subjunctive Use the subjunctive properly. If you are posing a hypothesis contrary to fact, you must use the subjunctive. *If I were you ...* or *If Hitler were alive today, he could tell us whether he kept a diary.*

If the hypothesis may or may not be true, you do not use the subjunctive. *If this diary is not Hitler's, we shall be glad we did not publish it.*

If you have *would* in the main clause, you must use the subjunctive in the *if* clause. *If you were to disregard this rule, you would make a fool of yourself.*

It is common nowadays to use the subjunctive in such constructions as:

He demanded that the Russians withdraw.

They insisted that the Americans also move back.

The referee suggested both sides cool it.

In soccer it is necessary that everyone remain civil.

This construction is correct, and has always been used in America, whence it has recrossed the Atlantic. In Britain, though, it fell into disuse some time ago except in more formal contexts:
I command the prisoner be summoned.
I beg that the motion be put to the house.

In British English, but not in American, a better course is to insert the word *should*:
He demanded that the Russians should withdraw.
The Americans should also move back.
Both sides should cool it.
Everyone should remain civil.

Alternatively (and best of all), some of the sentences could be rephrased:
He asked the Russians to withdraw.
It is necessary for everyone to remain civil.

See also **may and might.**

tenses Any account of events that have taken place must use a past tense. Yet newspaper articles may have greater immediacy if they use the present or future tenses where appropriate.

The perfect and pluperfect tenses also serve a purpose, often making accounts more pointed, and so more interesting. Here are a few rough rules:

1   If you use the past simple (aorist) tense, put a time or date to the event: *He died on April 11th.*
2   If you cannot, or do not want to, pin down the occasion in this way, use the perfect tense: *He has died,* or the present, *He is dead.* These imply continuance.
3   The pluperfect should be used for events that punctuate past continuance: *He grew up in post-war Germany, where he had seen the benefits of hard work.*

So does the imperfect tense: *He was a long time dying.*

See also **may and might.**

ground rules Just as *house rules* are the rules of the particular house, so *ground rules* are *the rules of the particular ground* (or grounds). They are not *basic* or *general rules.*

halve is a transitive verb, so deficits can double but not *halve*. They must *be halved* or *fall by half*.

haver means to *talk nonsense*, not *dither*, *swither* or *waver*.

headings and captions set the tone: they are more read than anything else, especially in a newspaper. Use them, therefore, to draw readers in, not to repel them. That means wit (where appropriate), not bad puns; sharpness (ditto), not familiarity (call people by last names, not first names); originality, not clichés.

Writers and editors, having laboured over an article, are too often ready to yank a well-known catchphrase, or the title of a film, from the front of their mind without giving the matter any more thought. They do so, presumably, in the belief that the heading is less important than the words beneath it. If you find yourself reaching for any of the following, think again:

back to the future
bridges (or anything else) too
   far
China syndromes
could do better (a
   favourite with education
   stories)
deal or no deal
empires striking back
flavours of the month
French connections
F-words
generation X

hearts and minds
kinder, gentler
mind the gap
new kids on the block
perfect storms
shaken, not stirred
$64,000 questions
southern discomfort
taxing times (tax stories)
thirty-somethings
where's the beef?
windows of opportunity

On October 18th 2004, for instance, an *Economist* reader wrote as follows:

> SIR – Your newspaper this week contains headlines derived from the following film titles: "As Good As It Gets", "Face-Off", "From Russia With Love", "The Man Who Planted Trees", "Up Close and Personal" and "The Way of the Warrior". Also employed are "the Iceman Cometh", "Measure for Measure", "The Tyger" and "War and Peace" – to say nothing of the old stalwart, "Howard's Way".
>
> Is this a competition, or do your sub-editors need to get out more?
>
> Tom Braithwaite,
> London

See also **clichés, journalese and slang.**

health care The American system of *health care* (adjective, *health-care*) for the poor is *Medicaid*, and for the elderly is *Medicare*. Canada's national health-care system is also called *Medicare*.

healthy If you think something is *desirable* or *good*, say so. Do not call it *healthy.*

heresy *see* **apostasy.**

heteronym *see* **homograph, homophone.**

hoards, hordes Few secreted treasures or stashes of things like food and money being kept to guard against privation (*hoards*) are multitudes on the move (*hordes*).

Hobson's choice is not *the lesser of two evils*; it is *no choice at all.*

holistic properly refers to a theory developed by Jan Smuts, who argued that, through creative evolution, nature tended to form wholes greater than the sum of the parts. If this is not what you mean by *holistic*, you would probably be wise to avoid it.

homeland Although it is now used as a synonym for the United States' domestic territory, your homeland is your *native land*, your *motherland* or even your *fatherland*.

homogeneous, homogenous *Homogeneous* means of the same kind or nature. *Homogenous* means similar because of common descent.

homograph, homophone *Homographs* are words with the same spelling but different meanings and sometimes different pronunciations. If they are spelt and pronounced the same they are also *homonyms*: *bear* (animal), *bear* (carry); *like* (similar), *like* (be fond of); *stalk* (part of a plant), *stalk* (to follow someone or something). If they are spelt the same but pronounced differently they are also *heteronyms*: *content* (happy), *content* (subject matter); *entrance* (way in), *entrance* (charm); *rebel* (to resist or fight against authority), *rebel* (someone who rebels).

Homophones are words that are pronounced the same regardless of how they are spelt and their meaning: *baited* (food put on a hook or trap), *bated* (diminished, restrained); *birth* (the process of bearing children); *berth* (somewhere to sleep in a ship, train etc); *heroin* (a Class A drug), *heroine* (a courageous woman).

homonym *see above.*

homosexual Since this word comes from the Greek word *homos* (same), not the Latin word *homo* (man), it applies as much to women as to men. It is therefore as daft to write *homosexuals and lesbians* as to write *people and women*.

hopefully Some authorities say it is pedantic and outmoded to object to the use of *hopefully* to mean *it is hoped that*. The practice originated in America, where English has been much influenced by German immigrants, who found the language of their new country had only one adverb to serve for both *hoffnungsvoll*, meaning full of hope, and *hoffentlich*, which can mean let's hope so. In *The Economist*, however, by all means begin an article hopefully, but do not write: *Hopefully, it will be finished by Wednesday*. Try *with luck, if all goes well, it is hoped that...*

horrible words Words that are horrible to one writer may not be
horrible to another, but if you are a writer for whom no words
are horrible, you would do well to take up some other activity.
No words or phrases should be banned outright from appearing
in print, but if you use any of the following you should be aware
that they may have an emetic effect on some of your readers.

carer – and most caring
expressions
chattering classes
facilitate
famously
governance
grow the business
guesstimate
informed (as in *his love of
language informed his memos*)
kids
likely (meaning *probably*,
rather than *probable*)

looking to (meaning *intending
to*)
materiel
ongoing
poster child
prestigious
proactive
rack up (profits, etc)
savvy
segue
showcase
source (meaning *obtain*)

See also **clichés.**

hyphens There is no firm rule to help you decide which words are
run together, hyphenated or left separate. If in doubt, consult
a dictionary. Do not overdo the literary device of hyphenating
words that are not usually linked: the stringing-together-of-lots-
and-lots-of-words-and-ideas tendency can be tiresome.

1 Words with common or short prefixes
In general, try to avoid putting hyphens into words formed
of one word and a short prefix.

3D
asexual
biplane
declassify
disfranchise
geopolitical
neoclassicism
neoconservative but
neo-cons

neoliberal
Neolithic
neologism
neonatal
overcapacity
overdone
overeducated
overemployment
precondition

predate	subcontinent
preoccupied	subcontract
preordained	subhuman
prepay	submachinegun
realign	suboptimal
rearm	subprime
rearrange	tetravalent
reborn	underdog
redirect	underdone
reopen	underinvest
reorder	underpaid
repurchase	upended
subcommittee	

2 Words beginning with re-
Some words that begin with *re* are hyphenated to avoid confusion:
re-cast
re-create (meaning create again)
re-present (meaning present again)
re-sort (meaning sort again)

3 Unfamiliar combinations
Words making unfamiliar combinations, especially if they would involve running consonants or vowels together, may benefit from a hyphen, so:
cross-reference (a cross reference would be unpleasant)
demi-paradise
over-governed
sub-investment grade
under-age
under-secretary

Antidisestablishmentarianism would, however, lose its point if it were hyphenated.

See also 5 below.

4 Fractions
Whether nouns or adjectives, these take hyphens:
one-half   one-sixth

four-fifths two-thirds

But note that it is *a half, a fifth, a sixth.*

5 Words that begin with

agri	infra	post
anti	inter	pre
counter	mid	semi
extra	multi	ultra
half	non	

The rules vary:

agri-business, agriculture

anti-aircraft, anti-fascist, anti-submarine (*but* antibiotic, anticlimax, antidote, antiseptic, antitrust)

counter-attack, counter-clockwise, counter-espionage, counter-intuitive (*but* counteract, countermand, counterpane)

extraordinary, extraterrestrial, extraterritorial (*but* extra-judicial)

half-baked, half-hearted, half-serious (*but* halfway)

infra-red

inter-agency, inter-country, inter-faith, inter-governmental, inter-regional (*but* intermediate, international, interpose)

mid-August, mid-week

multibillion, multilingual, multiracial (*but* multi-occupancy, multi-storey, multi-user)

non-combatant, non-existent, non-payment, non-violent (*but* nonaligned, nonconformist, nonplussed, nonstop)

postdate, post-war, pre-war

semi-automatic, semi-conscious, semi-detached

ultra-violet

6 The word *worth*
A sum followed by the word *worth* needs a hyphen: $25m-worth of goods.

7 Some titles

attorney-general	lieutenant-colonel	under-secretary
director-general	major-general	vice-president
field-marshal	secretary-general	

But:

deputy director	district attorney
deputy secretary	general secretary

8 Avoiding ambiguities
fine-tooth comb (most people do not comb their teeth)

a little-used car	a little used-car
third-world war	third world war
cross complaint	cross-complaint
high-school results	high school results

9 Aircraft

DC-10	MiG-23
Mirage F-1E	Lockheed P-3 Orion

(If in doubt, consult Jane's "All the World's Aircraft".)

Note that Airbus A340, BAe RJ70 do not have hyphens.

10 Calibres
The style for calibres is 50mm or 105mm with no hyphen, but 5.5-inch and 25-pounder.

11 Adjectives formed from two or more words
70-year-old judge
balance-of-payments difficulties
private-sector wages
public-sector borrowing requirement
right-wing groups (*but* the right wing of the party)
state-of-the-union message
value-added tax (VAT)

12 Adverbs
Adverbs do not need to be linked to participles or adjectives by hyphens in simple constructions:
The regiment was ill equipped for its task.
The principle is well established.
Though expensively educated, the journalist knew no grammar.

But if the adverb is one of two words together being used adjectivally, a hyphen may be needed:
The ill-equipped regiment was soon repulsed.
All well-established principles should be periodically challenged.

The hyphen is especially likely to be needed if the adverb is short and common, such as *ill*, *little*, *much* and *well*. Less common adverbs, including all those that end -ly, are less likely to need hyphens:
Never employ an expensively educated journalist.

13 Separating identical letters

book-keeping	re-emerge
coat-tails	re-entry
co-operate	side-effect
pre-eminent	trans-ship
pre-empt	unco-operative

Exceptions include:

overrate	overrun
overreach	skiing
override	underrate
overrule	withhold

14 Some nouns formed from prepositional verbs

bail-out	pay-off	shake-out
build-up	pull-out	shake-up
buy-out	rip-off	stand-off
call-up	round-up	start-up
get-together	run-up	trade-off
lay-off	set-up	

But:

fallout	lockout
handout	payout
knockout	turnout

15 The quarters of the compass

mid-west(ern)	south-east(ern)
north-east(ern)	south-west(ern)
north-west(ern)	

16 Hybrid ethnics
Greek-Cypriot, *Irish-American*, etc, whether noun or adjective.

17 Makers and making
A general, though not iron, rule for *makers* and *making*: if the

prefix is of one or two syllables, attach it without a hyphen to form a single word, but if the prefix is of three or more syllables, introduce a hyphen.

antimacassar-maker	clockmaker	steelmaker
bookmaker	holiday-maker	tiramisu-maker
candlestick-maker	lawmaker	troublemaker
carmaker	marketmaker	
chipmaker	peacemaker	

Policymaker and *profitmaking* are one word and an exception. But: note *foreign-policy maker (-ing).*

18 Other words ending *-er (-ing)* that are similar to *maker* and *making*

The general rule should be to insert a hyphen:

arms-trader	gun-runner
copper-miner	home-owner
drug-dealer	hostage-taker
drug-trafficker	mill-owner
field-worker	truck-driver
front-runner	vegetable-grower

But some prefixes, especially those of one syllable, can be used to form single words.

coalminer	metalworker	shipowner
farmworker	muckraker	steelworker
foxhunter	nitpicker (-ing)	steeplechaser
gatekeeper	peacekeeper	taxpayer
householder	shipbroker	
landowner	shipbuilder	

Less common combinations are better written as two words:

crossword compiler	gun owner
currency trader	insurance broker
dog owner	tuba player

19 Quotes

Words gathered together in quotation marks as adjectives do not usually need hyphens as well: *the "Live Free or Die" state.*

20 One word

airfield
airspace
airtime
bedfellow
bestseller (-ing)
bilingual
blackboard
blackout
blueprint
bookseller
businessman
bypass
cashflow (*but*
  cash flow in
  accountancy)
catchphrase
ceasefire
checklist
coastguard
codebreaker
comeback
commonsense
  (adj)
crossfire
cyberspace
dotcom
downturn
  (noun)
faultline
figleaf
fivefold
foothold
forever (adv,
  when pre-
  ceding verb)
foxhunter (-ing)
frontline (adj,
  but noun

front line)
girlfriend
goodwill
grassroots (adj
  and noun)
groundsman
halfhearted
halfway
handpicked
handwriting
hardline
headache
hijack
hobnob
kowtow
lacklustre
landmine
laptop
logjam
loophole
lopsided
lukewarm
machinegun
marketplace
minefield
nationwide
nevertheless
nonetheless
offline
offshore
oilfield
oilrig
online
onshore
peacetime
petrochemical
pickup truck
placename

rainforest
ringtone
roadblock
rustbelt
salesforce
seabed
shorthand
shortlist
shutdown
sidestep
soyabean
spillover
startup
statewide
stockmarket
streetwalker
strongman
sunbelt
takeover
threefold
threshold
timetable
trademark
transatlantic
transpacific
twofold
videocassette
videodisc
wartime
watchdog
website
whistleblower
windfall
workforce
worldwide
worthwhile

21 Two words

ad hoc
air base
air force
air strike
all right
any more
any time
arm's length
ballot box
birth rate
call centre
child care (noun)
cluster bombs
common sense (noun)
dare say
errand boy

for ever (when used after
  a verb)
health care (noun)
hedge fund
home page
joint venture
Land Rover
no one
photo opportunity
plea bargain
some day
some time
under way
vice versa
wild flowers (*but* adj.
  wildflower)

22 Two hyphenated words

aid-worker
aircraft-carrier
asylum-
  seekers
baby-boomer
balance-sheet
bell-ringer
break-even
climb-down
come-uppance
court-martial
  (noun and
  verb)
cross-border
cross-dresser
cross-sell
death-squads
derring-do
down-
  payment

drawing-board
end-game
end-year
faint-hearted
fund-raiser
  (-ing)
grown-up
hand-held
health-care
  (adj)
heir-apparent
home-made
hot-head
ice-cream
in-fighting
interest-group
kerb-crawler
know-how
laughing-stock
like-minded

long-standing
machine-tool
money-
  laundering
nation-
  building
nation-state
nest-egg
news-stand
number-plate
pot-hole
pressure-
  group
question-mark
rain-check
safety-valve
short-lived
starting-point
sticking-
  point

stumbling- block	think-tank	Wi-Max
subject-matter	time-bomb	window-
suicide-bomb	turning-point	dressing
(-er, -ing)	voice-over	wish-list
talking-shop	vote-winner	witch-hunt
task-force	war-chest	working-party
tear-gas	well-being	write-down
	Wi-Fi	(noun)

23 Three words
    ad hoc agreement (meeting, etc)   in so far
    armoured personnel carrier   multiple rocket launcher
    consumer price index   nuclear power station
    chief(s) of staff   sovereign wealth fund
    half a dozen   third world war (if things
    in as much   get bad)

24 Three hyphenated words
    A-turned-B (unless this leads to something unwieldy, so
    jobbing churchwarden turned captain of industry)
    brother-in-law   prisoners-of-war
    chock-a-block   second-in-command
    commander-in-chief   stock-in-trade
    no-man's-land

25 Numbers
    Avoid *from 1947–50* (say *in 1947–50* or *from 1947 to 1950*) and
    between 1961–65 (say *in 1961–65, between 1961 and 1965* or
    from 1961 to 1965). *See also* **figures.**

    "If you take hyphens seriously, you will surely go mad."
    (Oxford University Press style manual)

hypothermia is what kills old folk in winter. If you say it is
    hyperthermia, that means they have been carried off by heat
    stroke.

Icelandic names *see* **names.**

identical *with*, not *to*.

ilk means *same*, so *of that ilk* means *of the place of the same name as the family*, not *of that kind*. Best avoided.

immolate means to *sacrifice*, not to *burn*.

important If something is *important*, say why and to whom. Use sparingly, and avoid such unexplained claims as *this important house*, *the most important painter of the 20th century*. See also **interesting.**

impractical, impracticable If something is *impractical*, it is *not worth trying to do it*. If it's *impracticable*, it *cannot be done*. See also **practical, practicable.**

inchoate means *not fully developed* or *at an early stage*, not *incoherent* or *chaotic*.

including When *including* is used as a preposition, as it often is, it must be followed by a noun, pronoun or noun clause, not by a preposition. So *Iran needs more investment, including for its tired oil industry* is ungrammatical. The sentence should be rephrased, perhaps, as *Iran, including its tired oil industry, needs more investment*; or, *Iran needs more investment, especially for its tired oil industry*.

individual (noun) used occasionally, can be a useful colloquial term for *chap* or *bloke* or *guy* ("*In a corner, Parker, a grave, lean individual, bent over the chafing-dish, in which he was preparing for his employer and his guest their simple lunch.*" P.G. Wodehouse). Used indiscriminately as a term for person or, in the plural, *people*, it becomes bureaucratic ("*Individuals desiring to function as operators using instruments listed under paragraph (A)(3) of rule 3701–53–02 of the Administrative Code shall apply to the director of health for permits on forms prescribed and provided by the director of health.*" Ohio Department of Health).

Indonesian names *see* **names.**

initially Prefer *first, at first.*

interesting Like **important** and *funny, interesting* makes assumptions about the word or words it describes that may not be shared by the reader. Facts and stories introduced as interesting often turn out to be something else. "Interestingly, my father-in-law was born in East Kilbride," for instance. If something really is interesting, you probably do not need to say so.

inverted commas (quotation marks) *see* **punctuation.**

investigations of not *into.*

Iranian names *see* **names.**

Islamic, Islamist *Islamic* means relating to Islam; it is a synonym of the adjective *Muslim*, but it is not used for a follower of Islam, who is always *Muslim*. But *Islamic art and architecture* is conventional usage.

Islamist refers to those who see Islam as a political and social ideology as well as a religious one.

issues *The Economist* has issues – 51 a year – but if you think you have issues with *The Economist*, you probably mean you have *complaints, irritations* or *delivery problems*. If you disagree with *The Economist*, you may take issue with it. Do not use *issue* as a synonym for *problem.* Be precise.

Italian names *see* **names.**

italics

foreign words and phrases should be set in italics:

cabinet (French type)	*loya jirga*
de rigueur	*Mitbestimmung*
fatwa	*pace*
glasnost	*papabile*
Hindutva	*perestroika*
in camera	*persona non grata*
intifada	*sarariman*
jihad (and *jihadi*, but	*Schadenfreude*
jihadist)	*ujamaa*

If they are so familiar that they have become anglicised, they should be in roman. For example:

a priori	in absentia
à propos	in situ
ad hoc	machismo
apartheid	nom de guerre
avant-garde	nouveau riche
bête noire	parvenu
bona fide	pogrom
bourgeois	post mortem
café	putsch
chargé d'affaires	raison d'être
coup d'état (but *coup de*	Realpolitik
foudre, coup de grâce)	status quo
de facto, de jure	tsunami
dirigisme	vice versa
en masse, en route	vis-à-vis
grand prix	

Remember to put appropriate accents and diacritical signs on French, German, Spanish and Portuguese words in italics (and give initial capital letters to German nouns when in italics, but not if not). Make sure that the meaning of any foreign word you use is clear. *See also* **accents.**

For the Latin names of animals, plants, etc, *see* **spelling** and Part 3.

newspapers and periodicals Only *The Economist* has *The* italicised. Thus the *Daily Telegraph*, the *New York Times*, the *Financial Times*, the *Spectator* (but *Le Monde*, *Die Welt*, *Die Zeit*). The *Yomiuri Shimbun* should be italicised, but you can also say the *Yomiuri*, or the *Yomiuri* newspaper, as *shimbun* simply means newspaper in Japanese.

books, pamphlets, films, plays, operas, ballets, radio and television programmes Titles are roman, not italic, with capital letters for each main word, in quotation marks. Thus: "Pride and Prejudice", "Much Ado about Nothing", "Any Questions", "Crossfire", etc. But the Bible and its books (Genesis, Ecclesiastes, John, etc), as well as the Koran, are written without inverted commas. These rules apply to footnotes as well as bodymatter.

Web magazines and blogs are in italics, as for newspapers, with a lower-case "The" if appropriate.

headings, captions, cross-heads, rubrics Do not use italics.

lawsuits
Brown v Board of Education
Coatsworth v Johnson
Jarndyce v Jarndyce

If abbreviated, *versus* should always be shortened to *v*, with no point after it. The v should not be italic if it is not a lawsuit.

names of ships, aircraft, spacecraft
HMS Illustrious
Spirit of St Louis
Challenger
Air Force 1

algebraic formulae Thus: $e = mc^2$

Japanese names *see* **names.**

jib, gibe, gybe

jib (noun)	sail or boom of a crane
jib (verb)	to balk or shy
gibe (verb)	to scoff or flout
gibe (noun)	taunt
gybe (verb)	to alter course

Don't *jibe*.

jihad is the Arabic word for *struggle*. For modern Muslims, it may mean *military war* to propagate Islamism, that is, to spread Islam as a religious, political and social ideology (*jihad* of the sword). Or it may mean *spiritual striving* for personal purification and moral betterment (*jihad* against oneself). Or it may merely mean *doing right, improving society* and *being virtuous* (*jihad* of the tongue or of the hand). A religious obligation for all Muslims, *jihad* is for most a non-violent duty, though for some a violent one. Do not therefore use it simply to mean *holy war*, which it never did in classical Arabic. Rather, make clear what sort of *jihad* is under discussion in the context.

Someone engaged in *jihad* is a *mujahid* (plural, *mujahideen*) or a *jihadist* (*jihadi*). Logically, *mujahideen* and jihadists might be considered to be engaged in a struggle that could be either violent or non-violent. In practice, the terms nowadays are always used of Muslims engaged in an armed struggle, though *mujahideen* may simply be Muslim militants fighting for a cause, whereas jihadists are always fighting to spread Islamism by force.

journalese and slang Do not be too free with slang like *He really hit the big time in 2001.* Slang, like metaphors, should be used only occasionally if it is to have effect. Avoid expressions used only by journalists, such as giving people *the thumbs up, the thumbs down* or *the green light.* Stay clear of *gravy trains* and *salami tactics.* Do not use *the likes of,* or *Big Pharma (big drug firms).*

Try not to be predictable, especially predictably jocular. Spare your readers any mention of *mandarins* when writing about the civil service, of *their lordships* when discussing the House of Lords, and of *comrades* when analysing communist parties. Must all stories about Central Asia include a reference to the *Great Game?* Must all lawns be *manicured?* Must all small towns in the old confederacy be called the *buckle on the Bible belt?* Are drug-traffickers inevitably *barons?* Must starlets and models always be *scantily clad?* Is there any other kind of *wonk* than a *policy wonk?*

Resist saying *This will be no panacea.* When you find something that is indeed a *panacea* (or a *magic* or *silver bullet*), that will indeed be news. Similarly, hold back from offering the reassurance *There is no need to panic.* Instead, ask yourself exactly when there is a need to panic.

In general, try to make your writing fresh. It will seem stale if it reads like journalese. Prose such as this is often freighted with codewords (writers apply *respected* to someone they approve of, *militant* to someone they disapprove of, *prestigious* to something you won't have heard of). The story usually starts with *First the good news,* inevitably to be followed in due course by *Now the bad news.* An alternative is *Another week, another bomb* (giving rise to thoughts of *Another story, another hackneyed opening*). Or, *It was the best of times, it was the worst of times* – and certainly the feeblest of introductions (except when Dickens first thought of it). A quote will then be inserted, attributed to *one* (never *an*) *industry analyst,* and often the words *If, and it's a big if …* Towards the end, after an admission that the author has no idea what is going on, there is always room for *One thing is certain,* before rounding off the article with *As one wag put it …*

See also **clichés, headings and captions, metaphors.**

key A *key* may be *major* or *minor*, but not *low*. Few of the decisions, people, industries described as *key* are truly *indispensable*, and fewer still *open locks*.

This overused word is a noun and, like many nouns, may be used adjectivally (as in the *key ministries*). Do not, however, use it as a free-standing adjective, as in *The choice of running-mate is key*.

Do not use *key* to make the subject of your sentence more important than he, she or it really is. The words *key players* are a sure sign of a puffed-up story and a lazy mind.

Korean names *see* **names.**

Kyrgyzstan, Kirgiz *see* **placenames.**

lag If you *lag* transitively, you *lag a pipe* or *a loft*. Anything failing to keep up with a front-runner, rate of growth, fourth-quarter profit or whatever is *lagging behind it*.

last The *last* issue of *The Economist* implies its extinction; prefer *last week's* or the *latest* issue. *Last year*, in 2010, means 2009; if you mean the 12 months up to the time of writing, write the *past year*. The same goes for the *past* month, *past* week, *past* (not *last*) ten years. *Last week* is best avoided; anyone reading it several days after publication may be confused. *This week* is permissible.

Latin names When it is necessary to use a Latin name for animals, plants, etc, follow the standard practice. Thus for all creatures higher than viruses, write the binomial name in italics, giving an initial capital to the first word (the genus): *Turdus turdus*, the songthrush; *Metasequoia glyptostroboides*, the dawn redwood; *Culicoides clintoni*, a species of midge. This rule also applies to *Homo sapiens* and to such uses as *Homo economicus*. On second mention, the genus may be abbreviated (*T. turdus*). In some species, such as dinosaurs, the genus alone is used in lieu of a common name: *Diplodocus*, *Tyrannosaurus*. Also *Drosophila*, a fruitfly favoured by geneticists. But *Escherichia coli*, a bacterium also favoured by geneticists, is known universally as *E. coli*, even on first mention.

leverage If you really cannot find a way of avoiding the word *leverage*, you must explain what it means (unless it is simply *the use of a lever to gain a mechanical advantage*). In its technical sense, as a noun, it may mean *the ratio of long-term debt to total* *capital employed.* But note that *operating leverage* and *financial leverage* are different. The verb is even viler than the noun (try *lever). See also* **gearing**.

liberal in Europe, someone who believes above all in the freedom of the individual; in the United States, someone who believes in the progressive tradition of Franklin D. Roosevelt.

lifestyle Prefer *way of life.*

like, unlike govern nouns and pronouns, not verbs and clauses. So *as in America* not *like in America, as I was saying,* not *like I was saying, as Grandma used to make them,* not *like Grandma used to make them.* English has no word for the opposite of *as* that would be the equivalent of *unlike,* so you must rephrase the sentence if you are tempted to write *unlike in this context, unlike at Christmas,* or *unlike when I was a child.*

If you find yourself writing *She looked like she had had enough* or *It seemed like he was running out of puff,* you should replace *like* with *as if* or *as though,* and you probably need the subjunctive: *She looked as if she had had enough, It seemed as if he were running out of puff* (or, even better, *He seemed to be running out of puff*).

Ogden Nash reminds us that this infelicity, sadly, is nothing new:
Like the hart panteth for the water brooks I pant for a
revival of Shakespeare's "Like You Like It".
I can see tense draftees relax and purr
When the sergeant barks, "Like you were."
– And don't try to tell me that our well has been defiled
by immigration;
Like goes Madison Avenue, like so goes the nation.

But *authorities like Fowler and Gowers* is a perfectly acceptable alternative to *authorities such as Fowler and Gowers.*

likely Avoid such American constructions as *He will likely announce the date on Monday* and *The price will likely fall when results are posted Friday.* Prefer *He is likely to announce ...* or *It is likely that the price will ...* Or just use *probably.*

91

locate (in all its forms) can usually be replaced by something less ugly. *The missing scientist was located* means he was *found. The diplomats will meet at a secret location* means either that they will meet *in a secret place* or that they will meet *secretly. A company located in Texas* is simply *a company in Texas.*

lower case *see* **capitals.**

luxurious, luxuriant *Luxurious* means *indulgently pleasurable; luxuriant* means *exuberant* or *profuse.* A tramp may have a *luxuriant beard* but not a *luxurious life.*

masterful, masterly *Masterful* means *imperious; masterly* means *skilled.*

may and might are not always interchangeable, and you may want *may* more often than you think. If in doubt, try *may* first. *I might be wrong, but I think it will rain later* should be *I may be wrong, but I think it will rain later.*

Much of the trouble arises from the fact that *may* becomes *might* in both the subjunctive and in some constructions using past tenses. *Mr Blair admits that weapons of mass destruction may never be found* becomes, in the past, *Mr Blair admitted that weapons of mass destruction might never be found.*

Conditional sentences using the subjunctive also need *might.* Thus *If Sarah Palin were to write a novel, it might be called a thriller from Wasilla.* This could be rephrased by *If Sarah Palin writes a novel, it may be called a thriller from Wasilla.* Conditional sentences stating something contrary to fact, however, need *might: If pigs had wings, birds might raise their eyebrows.*

The facts are crucial. *New research shows Tutankhamun may have died of a broken leg* is fine, if indeed that is what the research shows. *New research shows Tutankhamun might have died of a broken leg* is not fine, unless it is followed by something like *if his mummy hadn't dressed the wound before it became infected.* This, though, is saying something quite different. In the first example, it is clear both that Tutankhamun died and that a broken leg may have been responsible. In the second, it is clear only that his wound was dressed; as a result, Tutankhamun seems to have survived.

Sometimes it is all right to use *might* if part of the sentence is understood though not explicitly stated: *Silvio Berlusconi would never tell a fib, but Jeffrey Archer might (if circumstances demanded or if he had forgotten the truth). That might be actionable (if a judge said it was).*

Facts remain crucial: *I might have called him a liar (but I didn't have the guts). I may have called him a liar (I can't now remember).*

Do not write *He might call himself an ardent free-market banker, but he did not reject a government rescue.* It should be *He may call himself an ardent free-market banker, but he did not reject a government rescue.* Only if you are putting forward a hypothesis that may or may not be true are may and might interchangeable. Thus *If he is honest with himself, he may (or might) call himself something else in future.*

Could is sometimes useful as an alternative to *may* and *might*: *His coalition could (or may) collapse.* But take care. Does *He could call an election in May* mean *He may call an election in May* or *He would be allowed to call an election in May*?

Do not use *may* or *might* when the appropriate verb is *to be*. *His colleagues wonder how far the prime minister may go. The danger for them is that they may all lose their seats* should be *His colleagues wonder how far the prime minister will go. The danger for them is that they will all lose their seats.*

See also **grammar and syntax.**

measures *see* Part 3.

media Prefer *press and television* or, if the context allows it, just *press*. If you have to use the *media*, remember they are plural.

meta- is a prefix derived from the Greek word for *with, beyond* or *after*, has long been used before the name of a science to designate what the Oxford English Dictionary calls a higher science of the same nature but dealing with ulterior problems, such as metachemistry, metaphysiology. This, says the OED, is done in supposed analogy to metaphysics, which is misapprehended as meaning the science of that which transcends the physical. Philosophers have extended the usage to, for example, metalanguage, language about language, which is used to express metatheorems, and computer geeks have fallen on it with delight, coining meta-elements, metadata, metatags. The practice of meta-naming is now adopted by those who wish to add scientific gravitas to almost any subject, especially any that is intrinsically jejune.

metaphors "A newly invented metaphor assists thought by evoking a visual image," said Orwell, "while on the other hand a metaphor which is technically 'dead' (eg, iron resolution) has in effect reverted to being an ordinary word and can generally be used without loss of vividness. But in between these two classes there is a huge dump of worn-out metaphors which are merely used because they save people the trouble of inventing phrases for themselves."

Every issue of *The Economist* contains scores of metaphors: gay soldiers booted back on to Civvy Street, asset-price bubbles pricked, house prices getting monetary medicine, gauntlets thrown down, ideas floated, tides turned, accounts embraced, barrages of criticism unleashed, retailing behemoths arriving with a splash, foundering chains, both floods and flocks of job-seekers, limelight hogged, inflation ignited, the ratio of chiefs to Indians, landmark patent challenges, drug giants taking steps towards the dark side, cash-strapped carmakers, football clubs teetering on the brink, prices inching up (or peaking, spiking or even going north), a leaden overhang of shares, giddying rises, rosy scenarios being painted, a fat lady not singing.

Some of these are tired, and will therefore tire the reader. Most are so exhausted that they may be considered dead. Dead or alive, take great care not to mix them.

An issue of *The Economist* chosen at random had: a package cutting the budget deficit, the administration loath to sign on to higher targets, the lure of eastern Germany as a springboard to the struggling markets of eastern Europe, west Europeanness helping to dilute an image, someone finding a pretext to stall the process before looking for a few integrationist crumbs, a spring clean that became in the next sentence a stalking-horse for greater spending, and Michelin axing jobs in painful surgery.

Within four consecutive sentences in another issue lay: a chance to lance the Israel-Palestine boil, Americans and Europeans sitting on their hands while waiting for Israel to freeze settlement building, or for Palestinians to corral militants, the need to stop the two sides playing the "after you" game, a confidence-building and money-begging conference followed by a shot in the arm for the Americans.

mete You may *mete out* punishment, but if it is to fit the crime it is *meet*.

metrics are the *theory of measurement*. Do not use the term as a pretentious word for *figures*, *dimensions* or *measurements* themselves, as in "*I can't take the metrics I'm privileged to and work my way to a number in [that] range*" (General George Metz, talking about the number of insurgents killed in Iraq).

migrate is intransitive. Do not *migrate people* or *things*.

millionaire The time has long gone when young women would think that the term *millionaire* adequately described the man who broke the bank at Monte Carlo. If you wish to use it, make it plain that *millionaire* refers to income (in dollars or pounds), not to capital. Otherwise try *plutocrat* or *rich man*.

mitigate, militate *Mitigate* mollifies or makes better; *militate* tells against.

monopoly, monopsony A *monopolist* is the sole seller. A sole buyer is a *monopsonist*. *See* **oligopoly**.

moot in British English means *arguable*, *doubtful* or *open to debate*. Americans often use it to mean *hypothetical* or *academic*, ie, *of no practical significance*. Prefer the British usage.

mortar If not a *vessel* in which herbs, etc, are pounded with a pestle, a *mortar* is a *piece of artillery* for throwing a shell, bomb or lifeline. Do not write *He was hit by a mortar* unless you mean he was struck by the artillery piece itself, which is improbable.

move Do not use *move* (noun) if you mean *decision, bid, deal* or something more precise. But *move* (verb) rather than *relocate*.

mujahid, mujahideen *see jihad*.

musical notes should be set in ordinary caps, thus: *Bach's* "Air on a G-string".

named *after*, not *for*.

names

For guidance on spelling people's names, see the list below. As with all names, spell them the way the person concerned has requested, if a preference has been expressed. Here are some names that cause spelling difficulties:

Akbar Hashemi Rafsanjani
Alain Lamassoure
Alexander Solzhenitsyn
Alyaksandr Lukashenka
Andrei Sakharov
Andrej Olechowski
Arnold Schwarzenegger
Atal Behari Vajpayee
Aung San Suu Kyi (Miss Suu Kyi)
Banharn Silpa-archa
Bashar Assad
Binyamin Netanyahu
Bob Kerrey (Nebraska)
Burhanuddin Rabbani
Carlo De Benedetti
Carlo Ripa di Meana
Ciriaco De Mita
Condoleezza Rice
Costas Karamanlis
Cuauhtémoc Cardenas

Cyril Ramaphosa
Daniel arap Moi
Deniz Baykal
Eduard Shevardnadze
Emile Lahoud
Felipe González
François Mitterrand
Franz Müntefering
Fyodor Dostoyevsky
Gaafar Numeiri
Gandhi
Gennady Zyuganov
Gerhard Schröder
Gianni De Michelis
Goodwill Zwelithini
Grigory Yavlinsky
Habsburg
Hans van den Broek (Mr Van den Broek)
Haris Silajdic
Issaias Afwerki (Mr Issaias)

Javier Solana
Jean Tiberi
Jean-Pierre Chevènement
Joaquín Almunia
John Kerry (Massachusetts)
José Luis Rodríguez Zapatero
(Mr Zapatero)
José Manuel Barroso (no
need to include his third
name, Durão)
José María Aznar
José Sócrates
Josep Lluis Carod-Rivera
Juan José Ibarretxe
Kim Dae-jung
Kim Jong Il
King Mohammed of Morocco
Leopoldo Calvo-Sotelo
Luiz Inácio (Lula) da Silva
Mahathir Mohamad (Dr)
Mangosuthu Buthelezi
Mikhail Gorbachev
Mikheil Saakashvili
Milan Martic
Milan Mrsic
Mohammed Zahir Shah
Muammar Qaddafi
Muhammad (unless it is part
of the name of someone
who spells it differently)
Mullah Mohammed Omar

Nicolae Ceausescu
Nicolas Sarkozy
Nikita Khrushchev
Nursultan Nazarbayev
Otto Schily
Prince Ranariddh
Radovan Karadzic
Ratko Mladic
Recep Tayyip Erdogan
Reichmann brothers
Ritt Bjerregaard
Robert Schumann (composer)
Rodrigo de Rato (Mr de Rato)
Sergei Kozalev
Slobodan Milosevic
Tabaré Vázquez (Dr)
Traian Basescu
Valéry Giscard d'Estaing
Velupillai Prabhakaran
Viktor Pynzenyk
Viktor Tymoshenko
Viktor Yushchenko
Vladimir Zhirinovsky
Vojislav Kostunica
Wlodzimierz Cimoszewicz
Wolfgang Schäuble
Yasser Arafat
Yitzhak Rabin
Yitzhak Shamir
Yulia Tymoshenko
Yves-Thibault de Silguy

See also specific listings below.

Afghan

Gulbuddin Hikmatyar
Ahmad Shah Masoud
Mullah Mohammed Omar

Burhanuddin Rabbani
Mazar-i-Sharif

Arabic names and words

Al, al- Try to leave out the *Al*, *Al-*, *al* or *al-*. This is common practice with well-known figures like Bashar Assad (not al-Assad) and Muammar Qaddafi (not al-Qaddafi). Many names, however, would look peculiar without *al-*, so with less well-known people it should be included (lower case, usually followed by a hyphen). On subsequent mentions, it can be dropped. *Bin* (son of) must be repeated: *Osama bin Laden*, thereafter *Mr bin Laden.* But it is often ignored in alphabetisation.

The *Al-*, *Al-*, *al* or *al-* (or *Ad-*, *Ar-*, *As-*, etc) before most Arab towns can be dropped (so *Baquba* not *al-Baquba*, *Ramadi* not *ar-Ramadi*). But *al-Quds* because it is the Arab name for Jerusalem and will be important in any context in which it appears.

Some common Arabic names are:

Abdel Aziz (founder of
   Kingdom of Saudi)
Abdel Halim Khaddam
Abdullah, King
Abu Alaa (aka Ahmed Queri)
Abu Mazen (aka Abbas)
Abu Musab al-Zarpawi
Adel abd al-Mahdi
Ahmad Jibril
Ahmed Chalabi
Ahmed Queri
Al Saud (*not* al-Saud, since
   the Al in this instance
   means house of)
Ali Abdullah Saleh
Ali al-Sistani (Grand
   Ayatollah)
al-Qaeda
Amin Gemayel
Anwar Sadat
Bahrain
Barham Saleh

Bashar Assad
Boutros Boutros-Ghali
Chouf (the)
Farouq Qaddoumi
Gaza Strip (and City)
Hafez Assad
Hassan, Crown Prince
Hizbullah
Hosni Mubarak
Hussein, King
Ibn Khaldoun
Ibrahim al-Jaafari (Dr)
Islamic Jihad
Iyad Allawi
Jaafar Numeiri
Jalal Talabani
jamaat islamiya
Jeddah
King Fahd
Maronite
Marwan Barghouti
Masjid Sulayman

Masoud Barzani
Mohamed ElBaradei
Mohammed al-Maktoum
Mosul
Muammar Qaddafi
Muhammad Dahlan
Muhammad the Prophet
Mukhabarat
Muqtada al-Sadr
Mustafa Barghouti
Nuri al-Maliki
Omar Al-Bashir
Qaboos, Sultan
Rafik Hariri
Ras Tanura
Riyadh
Sabah al-Ahmad, Sheikh
Saddam Hussein
Sadiq el-Mahdi
Salam Fayyad

Samarra
Sana'a
Saud al-Faisal, Prince
Saud ibn Abdel Aziz (king of
    Saudi Arabia who followed
    Abdel Aziz)
Sharjah
Sharm el Sheikh
Shatt al-Arab
Strait of Hormuz
Suleiman Franjieh
Tal Afar
Tawheed
Umm al Aish
Wahhabi
Walid Jumblatt
Yasser Arafat
Zayed, Sheikh
Zine el-Abidine Ben Ali

And some common Arabic words are:
burqa   *Hizbullah*
Fatah   *hudna*
Hadith   *intifada*
hajj   *niqab*
hijab

See also **Arabic**.

Bangladeshi If the name includes the Islamic definite article, it should be lower case and without any hyphens: *Mujib ur Rahman.*

Belarusian If *Belarusians* (not *Belarussians*) wish to be known by the Belarusian form of their names (*Ihor, Vital*), so be it. But use the familiar, Russian, placenames (*Minsk*, not *Miensk*), and *Alexander Lukashenko.*

Cambodian On second reference, repeat both names, adding *Mr*: *Mr Hun Sen, Mr Sam Rainsy.*

Central Asian For those with Russified names, *see* **Russian**.

Askar Akayev	Nursultan Nazarbayev
Heidar Aliyev	Saparmurat Niyazov

Chinese In general, follow the pinyin spelling of Chinese names, which has replaced the old Wade-Giles system, except for people from the past, and people and places outside mainland China. *Peking* is therefore *Beijing* and *Mao* is *Zedong*, not *Tse-tung*.

There are no hyphens in pinyin spelling. So:

Deng Xiaoping	Qingdao (Tsingtao)
Guangdong (Kwangtung)	Tianjin (Tientsin)
Guangzhou (Canton)	Xi Jinping
Jiang Qing (Mrs Mao)	Xinjiang (Sinkiang)
Mao Zedong (Tse-tung)	Zhao Ziyang

But:

Chiang Kai-shek	Li Ka-shing
Hong Kong	Lee Teng-hui

The family name comes first, so *Xi Jinping* becomes *Mr Xi* on a later mention.

Note that *Peking University* and *Tsinghua University* have kept their pre-pinyin romanised names.

Dutch If using first name and surname together, *vans* and *dens* are lower case: *Dries van Agt* and *Joop den Uyl*. But without their first names they become *Mr Van Agt* and *Mr Den Uyl*; *Hans van den Broek* becomes *Mr Van den Broek*. These rules do not always apply to Dutch names in Belgium and South Africa: *Herman Van Rompuy* (thereafter *Mr Van Rompuy*); *Karel Van Miert* (*Mr Van Miert*).

Note that *Flemings* speak *Dutch*.

French Any *de* is likely to be lower case, unless it starts a sentence. *De Gaulle* goes up; *Charles de Gaulle* and plain *de Gaulle* go down. So does *Yves-Thibault de Silguy*.

German Any *von* is likely to be upper case only at the start of a sentence.

Icelandic Most Icelanders do not have family names. They take their last name from the first name of their father, so *Leifur Eiriksson*, say, is the son of *Eirikur*, and *Freyja Haraldsdottir* is the daughter of *Harald*. If she marries Leifur Eiriksson, she continues to be known as Freyja Haraldsdottir, their son has Leifsson as his last name (patronym) and their daughter Leifsdottir. Both names (or more, if someone has two first names) should be used on first and all subsequent references (when they should be preceded by Mr, Mrs or the appropriate title). A few Icelanders, such as the late *President Kristjan Eldjarn*, do have family names. These are the only people who can be referred to by one name only.

Indonesian Generally straightforward, but:

Abu Bakar Basyir   Muhammadiyah   Syafii Maarif
Jemaah Islamiah   Nahdlatul Ulama

Some Indonesians have only one name. On first mention give it to them unadorned: *Budiono*. Thereafter add the appropriate title: *Mr Budiono*. For those who have several names, be sure to get rid of the correct ones on second and subsequent mentions:

Susilo Bambang Yudhoyono, for example, becomes President (or Mr) Yudhoyono.

President Joko Widodo is so popularly known as Jokowi that he should be referred to as Jokowi after the first mention.

Iranian *Farsi*, an Arabised version of *Parsi* (meaning *of Persia*), is the term Iranians use for their language. In English, the language is properly called *Persian*.

The language spoken in Iran (and Tajikistan) is *Persian*, not *Farsi*.

Here is a list of some words and proper names.

Abadan	*baseej*
Abu Musa	Bushehr
Mahmoud Ahmadinejad	Hojjatieh
Ahwaz	Kermanshah
Ali Akbar Velayati	Keyhan
Bahai	Ali Khamenei, Ayatollah
Bandar Abbas	Kharg island

Muhammad Khatami	Rezaiyeh
Bandar Khomeini	Hassan Rohani
Khorramshahr	Yusef Saanei, Ayatollah
Khuzestan	Abdolkarim Soroush
Lavan island	Strait of Hormuz
Mahdavi-Kani, Ayatollah	Jalaluddin Taheri, Ayatollah
maqnaeh	Taqi Banki
Hossein-Ali Montazeri,	Tehran
Ayatollah	Tudeh
Hossein Moussavi	Tumbs
Queshm	*velayet-e faqih*
Akbar Hashemi Rafsanjani	Yahyaoui
Massoud Rajavi	

Italian Any *De* is likely to be upper case, but there are exceptions (especially among aristocrats such as *Carlo Ripa di Meana*), so check.

Japanese Although the Japanese put the family name first in their own language (*Koizumi Junichiro*), they generally reverse the order in western contexts. So: Junichiro Koizumi, Heizo Takenaka, Shintaro Ishihara, etc.

Korean South Koreans have changed their convention from *Kim Dae Jung* to *Kim Dae-jung*. But North Koreans, at least pending unification, have stuck to *Kim Jong Il*. Kim is the family name.

The South Korean party formed in 2003 is the Uri Party.

Pakistani If the name includes the Islamic definite article *ul*, it should be lower case and without any hyphens: *Zia ul Haq*, *Mahbub ul Haq* (but *Sadruddin*, *Mohieddin* and *Saladin* are single words).

The genitive *e* is hyphenated: *Jamaat-e-Islami, Muttahida Majlis-e-Amal*.

Russian Each approach to transliterating Russian has drawbacks. The following rules aim for phonetic accuracy, except when that conflicts with widely accepted usage.

No *y* before *e* after consonants: *Belarus, perestroika, Oleg, Lev, Medvedev.* (The actual pronunciation is somewhere between *e* and *ye*.)

1 Where pronunciation dictates, put a *y* before the *a* or *e* at the start of a word or after a vowel:

Aliyev *not* Aliev   Dostoyevsky
Baluyevsky   Yavlinsky
Dudayev   Yevgeny *not* Evgeny

2 Words spelled with *e* in Russian but pronounced *yo* should be spelled *yo*. Thus:

Fyodorov *not* Fedorov
Pyotr *not* Petr
Seleznyov *not* Seleznev

But stick to *Gorbachev, Khrushchev* and other famous ones that would otherwise look odd.

3 With words that could end *-i, -ii, -y* or *-iy*, use *-y* after consonants and *-i* after vowels. This respects both phonetics and common usage.

Georgy   Yury
Gennady   Zhirinovsky
Nizhny

But:
Bolshoi   Rutskoi
Nikolai   Sergei

Exception (because conventional): *Tolstoy*.

4 Replace *dzh* with *j*.
Jokhar, Jugashvili (for Stalin; bowing to convention, give his first name as *Josef*, not Iosif).

5 Prefer *Aleksandr, Viktor, Eduard, Piotr* to Alexander, Victor, Edward, Peter, unless the person involved has clearly chosen an anglicised version. But keep the familiar spelling for historical figures such as *Alexander Nevsky, Alexander Solzhenitsyn* and *Peter the Great*.

Singaporean names have no hyphens and the family name comes first: *Lee Kuan Yew* (thereafter *Mr Lee*).

Spanish Spaniards sometimes have several names, including two surnames. On first mention, spell out in full all the names of such people, if they use both surnames. Thereafter the normal practice is to write the first surname only, so *Joaquín Almunia Amann* becomes *Mr Almunia* on second and subsequent mentions.

Often, though, the second surname is used only by people whose first surname is common, such as *Fernández*, *López* or *Rodríguez*. To avert confusion with others, they may choose to keep both their surnames when they are referred to as Mr This or Mr That, so *Miguel Ángel Fernández Ordóñez*, for instance, becomes *Mr Fernández Ordóñez*, just as *Andrés Manuel López Obrador* becomes *Mr López Obrador* and *Juan Fernando López Aguilar* becomes *Mr López Aguilar*. A few people, notably *José Luis Rodríguez Zapatero*, choose to have their names shortened to just the second of their surnames, so he becomes *Mr Zapatero*.

Although on marriage Spanish women sometimes informally add their husband's name (after a *de*) to their own, they do not usually change their legal name, merely adopting *Señora* in place of *Señorita*. Unless the woman you are writing about prefers some other title, you should likewise simply change from *Miss* to *Mrs*.

Swiss personal names follow the rules for the two languages mostly spoken in Switzerland: French and German.

Turk, Turkic, Turkmen, Turkoman, etc *see* **placenames.**

Ukrainian After an orgy of retransliteration from their Russian versions, a convention has emerged. Its main rules are these.

1 Since Ukrainian has no g, use *h*: *Hryhory, Heorhy, Ihor* (not *Grigory, Georgy, Igor*). Exception: *Georgy Gongadze*.
2 Render the Ukrainian i as an i, and the И as a y. So *Vital, Kharkiv, Chernivtsi*; but *Volodymyr, Yanukovych, Tymoshenko*,

Borys, Zhytomyr. Change words ending *-iy* to *-y* (*Hryhory*).

However, respect the wishes of those Ukrainians who wish to be known by their Russian names, or by an anglicised transliteration of them: *Alexander Morozov.*

Kiev remains *Kiev*, not *Kyiv*.

Vietnamese names have no hyphens and the family name comes first:
Ho Chi Minh
Tran Duc Luong (thereafter Mr Tran)

See also **placenames.**

neither ... nor *see* **none.**

new words and new uses for old words Part of the strength and vitality of English is its readiness to welcome new words and expressions, and to accept new meanings for old words. Yet such meanings and uses often depart as quickly as they arrived, and early adopters risk looking like super-trendies if they bring them into service too soon. Moreover, to anyone of sensibility some new words are more welcome than others, even if no two people of sensibility would agree on which words should be ushered in and which kept firmly on the doorstep.

Before grabbing the latest usage, ask yourself a few questions. Is it likely to pass the test of time? If not, are you using it to show just how cool you are? Has it already become a cliché? Does it do a job no other word or expression does just as well? Does it rob the language of a useful or well-liked meaning? Is it being adopted to make the writer's prose sharper, crisper, more euphonious, easier to understand – in other words, better? Or to make it seem more with it (yes, that was cool once, just as cool is cool now), more pompous, more bureaucratic or more politically correct – in other words, worse?

See also **clichés, horrible words, jargon, journalese and slang.**

none usually takes a singular verb. So does *neither* (or *either*) *A nor* (*or*) *B*, unless B is plural, as in *Neither the Dutchman nor the Danes* *have done it,* where the verb agrees with the element closest to it. Similarly,

> Come live with me and be my love,
> And we will all the pleasures prove
> That hills and valleys, dales and fields,
> Or woods or steepy mountain yields.
> (Christopher Marlowe)

nor means *and not,* so should not be preceded by *and.*

offensive In Britain, *offensive* (as an adjective) means *rude*; in
America, it often means *attacking*. Similarly, to the British an
offence is usually a *crime* or *transgression*; to Americans it is often
an *offensive*, or the counterpart to a *defence*.

oligopoly Limited competition between a small number of
producers or sellers. *See also* **monopoly, monopsony**.

one Try to avoid *one* as a personal pronoun. *You* will often do
instead.

only Put *only* as close as you can to the words it qualifies. Thus
These animals mate only in June. To say *They only mate in June*
implies that in June they do nothing else.

onto *On* and *to* should be run together when they are closely
linked, as in *He pranced onto the stage.* If, however, the sense of
the sentence makes the *on* closer to the preceding word, or the *to*
closer to the succeeding word, than they are to each other, keep
them separate: *He pranced on to the next town* or *He pranced on to
wild applause.*

overwhelm means *submerge utterly, crush, bring to sudden ruin.*
Majority votes, for example, seldom do any of these things.
As for the ethnic Albanians in Kosovo, although 90% of the
population, they turned out to be an *overwhelmed majority*, not
an *overwhelming one*, until NATO stepped in.

oxymoron An *oxymoron* is not an unintentional contradiction in terms but *a figure of speech in which contradictory terms are deliberately combined, as in: bitter-sweet, cruel kindness, friendly fire, jolie laide, open secret, sweet sorrow,* etc.

Pakistani names *see* **names.**

palate, pallet, palette Your *palate*, the roof of your mouth (or your capacity to appreciate food and drink), is best not confused with a *pallet*, a mattress on which you may sleep or a wooden frame for use with fork-lift trucks, still less with a *palette*, on which you may mix paints.

panacea Universal remedy. Beware of cliché usage. *See also* **journalese and slang.**

parliaments Do not confuse one part of a parliament with the whole thing. The Dail is only the lower house of Ireland's parliament, as the Duma is of Russia's and the Lok Sabha is of India's.

partner is useful for those who value gender-neutrality above all else, but others may prefer *boyfriend* or *girlfriend* or even *lover*. And remember that, if you take a *partner for the Gay Gordons*, you may not end up in bed together – just as lawyers and accountants and others *in partnerships* are not necessarily fornicating, even if they are *sleeping partners*.

passive *see* **grammar and syntax** (active, not passive).

peer (noun) is one of those words beloved of sociologists and eagerly co-opted by journalists who want to make their prose seem more authoritative. A *peer* is not a *contemporary, colleague* or *counterpart* but an *equal*.

per capita is the Latin for by heads; it is a term used by lawyers when distributing an inheritance among individuals, rather than among families (*per stirpes*). Unless the context demands this technical expression, never use either *per capita* or *per caput* but *per head* or *per person. See also* figures.

per cent is not the same as a *percentage point*. Nothing can fall, or be devalued, by more than 100%. If something trebles, it increases by 200%. If a growth rate increases from 4% to 6%, the rate is two percentage points or 50% faster, not 2%. *See also* **figures**.

percolate means to pass *through*, not *up* or *down*.

placenames In most contexts favour simplicity over precision and use Britain rather than Great Britain or the United Kingdom, and America rather than the United States. ("In all pointed sentences, some degree of accuracy must be sacrificed to conciseness." Dr Johnson)

Sometimes, however, it may be important to be precise. Remember therefore that *Great Britain* consists of *England, Scotland* and *Wales*, which together with *Northern Ireland* (which we generally call *Ulster*, though Ulster strictly includes three counties in *Ireland*) make up the *United Kingdom*.

Americans: Remember too that, although it is usually all right to talk about the inhabitants of the United States as *Americans*, the term also applies to everyone from Canada to Cape Horn. In a context where other North, Central or South American countries are mentioned, you should write *United States* rather than *America* or *American*, and it may even be necessary to write *United States citizens*.

EU is now well enough known (like the UN) to need no spelling out on first mention as the *European Union. Europe* and *Europeans* may sometimes be used as shorthand for citizens of countries of the European Union, but be careful: there are plenty of other Europeans too.

Europe: Note that although the place is *western* (or *eastern*) *Europe*, euphony dictates that the people are *west* (or *east*) *Europeans*.

Holland, though a nice, short, familiar name, is strictly only two of the 12 provinces that make up *the Netherlands*, and the *Dutch* do not like the misuse of the shorter name. So use *the Netherlands*.

Belgian placenames should be *Dutch* or *French* according to which part they are in.

Ireland is simply *Ireland*. Although it is a republic, it is not the Republic of Ireland. Neither is it, in English, Eire.

Madagascar: *Malagasy* is its adjective and the name of the inhabitants.

Scandinavia is primarily Norway and Sweden, but the term is often used to include Denmark, Iceland, Norway and Sweden, which, with Finland, make up the *Nordic countries*.

USA and *US* are not to be used (if they were they would spatter the paper), except in charts, as part of an official name (eg, *US Steel*), and sparingly in the Americas section to differentiate official bodies (the *US Border Patrol*).

Do not use the names of capital cities as synonyms for their governments. *Britain will send a gunboat* is fine, but *London will send a gunboat* suggests that this will be the action of the people of London alone. To write *Washington and Moscow now differ only in their approach to Havana* is absurd.

Washington, DC may shed the *DC* wherever there is no risk of confusion with Washington state, which is most of the time.

Note that a country is *it*, not *she*.

changes of name Where countries have made it clear that they wish to be called by a new (or an old) name, respect their requests. Thus:

Burkina Faso	Thailand
Myanmar	Zimbabwe
Sri Lanka	

Zaire has now reverted to *Congo*. In contexts where there can be no confusion with the ex-French country of the same name, plain *Congo* will do. But if there is a risk of misunderstanding, call it the *Democratic Republic of Congo* (never DRC). The other Congo can be *Congo-Brazzaville* if necessary. The river is now also the *Congo*. The people of either country are also *Congolese*.

Former Soviet republics that are now independent countries include:
Belarus (*not* Belorus or Belorussia), Belarusian (adjective)
Kazakhstan
Moldova (*not* Moldavia)
Tajikistan
Turkmenistan (*see* Turk, Turkic, Turkmen, Turkoman, page 118)

Kyrgyzstan is the name of the country. Its adjective is *Kyrgyzstani*, which is also the name of one of its inhabitants. But *Kirgiz* is the noun and adjective of the language, and the adjective of Kirgiz people outside Kyrgyzstan.

Follow local practice when a country changes the names of rivers, towns, etc, within it. Thus:
Almaty *not* Alma Ata
Chemnitz *not* Karl-Marx-Stadt
Chennai *not* Madras
Chernigov *not* Chernihiv
Chur *not* Coire
Kolkata *not* Calcutta
Lvov *not* Lviv
Mumbai *not* Bombay
Nizhny Novgorod *not* Gorky
Papua *not* Irian Jaya
Polokwane *not* Pietersburg
St Petersburg *not* Leningrad
Tshwane is the new name for the area around Pretoria but not yet for the city itself.
Yangon *not* Rangoon

However, the previous form should be preserved in historical contexts (the *Black Hole of Calcutta*). If the names are very dissimilar, add (*now xx*).

definite article Do not use the definite article before:

Krajina   Sudan
Lebanon   Transkei
Piedmont   Ukraine
Punjab

But:

Los Angeles   Le Havre
the Caucasus   the Maghreb
the Gambia   the Netherlands
The Hague   La Paz

English forms are preferred when they are in common use:

Andalusia   Ivory Coast
Archangel (*not* Archangelsk   Kiev
  or Arkhangelsk)   Leghorn
Cassel (*not* Kassel)   Majorca
Castile   Milan
Catalonia (catalan)   Minorca
Cologne   Minsk
Cordoba   Munich
Corinth   Naples
Corunna   Nuremberg
Cracow   Odessa
Dagestan   Pomerania
Dnieper   Salonika (*not* Thessaloniki)
Dniester (*but* Transdniestria)   Saragossa
Dusseldorf (*not* Düsseldorf)   Saxony (*and* Lower Saxony,
East Timor   Saxony-Anhalt)
Florence   Sebastopol
Geneva   Seville
Genoa   Turin
Hanover   Zurich (*not* Zürich)

Use British English rather than American – *Rockefeller Centre*, *Pew Centre for Research* – unless the placename is part of a company's name, such as *Rockefeller Center Properties Inc.*

The final s sometimes added by English-speakers to *Lyon*, *Marseille* and *Tangier* now seems precious, so use the s-less form.

some spellings

Abkhazia

Ajaria (*not* Adjaria)

Argentina (adj and people
 Argentine, *not*
 Argentinian)

Ashgabat

Azerbaijan

Baden-Württemberg

Baghdad

Bahamas (Bahamian)

Bahrain

Basel

Belarus

Bengalooru

Beqaa

Bermuda, Bermudian

Bern

Bophuthatswana

Bosporus (not Bosphorus)

British Columbia

Brittany, Breton (*but* Britannia,
 Britannic)

Cameroon

Cape Town

Caribbean

Catalan

Chechnya

Cincinnati

Colombia (South America)

Columbia (university, District
 of British)

the Comoros

Czech Republic; Czech Lands

Dar es Salaam

Derry/Londonderry (use
 in this full dual form at
 least on first mention;
 afterwards, plain Derry
 will do)

Dhaka

Djibouti

Dominica (Caribbean island)

Dominican Republic (part of
 another island)

El Salvador, Salvadorean

Falkland Islands (*not*
 Malvinas)

Falluja

Gaza Strip (*but* Gaza City)

Gettysburg

Gothenburg

Grozny

Guantánamo

Gujarat, Gujarati

Guyana (*but* French Guiana)

Gweru (*not* Gwelo)

Hanover

Hercegovina

Hong Kong (unless part of the
 name of a company which
 spells it as one word)

Ingushetia

Issyk-Kul

Ivory Coast, Ivorian

Jeddah

KaNgwane

Kathmandu

Kinmen (*not* Quemoy)

Kolkata

Kuwait City

KwaNdebele

KwaZulu-Natal

Kwekwe (*not* Que Que)

Laos, Lao (*not* Laotian)

Ljubljana
Londonderry (Derry also
   permissible)
Luhansk
Luxembourg
Lyon
Macau
Mafikeng
Mauritania
Middlesbrough
Mpumalanga (formerly
   Eastern Transvaal)
Mumbai (not Bombay)
Nagorno-Karabakh
Nepal, Nepali (not Nepalese)
New York City
north Caucasus
North Rhine-Westphalia
Ouagadougou
Philippines (the people are
   Filipinos and Filipinas)
Phnom Penh
Pittsburgh
Port-au-Prince
Putumayo
Pyrenees, Pyrenean
Quebec, Quebecker (but Parti
   Québécois)
Reykjavik

Rheims
Romania
Rwanda, Rwandan (not
   Rwandese)
St Petersburg
Salonika (not Thessaloniki)
Sana'a
Sea of Japan (East Sea) (give
   both names thus)
Salzburg
São Paulo
Sindh
Srebrenica
Strasbourg
Suriname
Taipei
Tehran
Teesside
Tigray, Tigrayan
Timbuktu
Transdniestra
Uffizi
Uzbekistan
Valletta
Yangzi
Zepa
Zepce
Zurich

See also **capitals** (places).

Turk, Turkic, Turkmen, Turkoman, etc
Turk, Turkish: noun and adjective of Turkey.

Turkoman, Turkomans: member, members, of a branch of the Turkish race mostly living in the region east of the Caspian sea once known as Turkestan and parts of Iran and Afghanistan; *Turkoman* may also be the language of the Turkmen and an adjective.

Turkic: adjective applied to one of the branches of the Ural-Altaic family of languages – Uighur, Kazan Tatar, Kirgiz.

Turkmen: Turkoman or Turkomans living in Turkmenistan; adjective pertaining to them.

Turkmenistani: adjective of Turkmenistan; also a native of that country.

plants For the spelling of the Latin names of animals, plants, etc, *see* **Latin names.**

plurals *see* **spelling.** For plural nouns, *see* **grammar and syntax.**

political correctness Avoid, if you can, giving gratuitous offence (*see* **euphemisms**): you risk losing your readers, or at least their goodwill, and therefore your arguments. But pandering to every plea for politically correct terminology may make your prose unreadable, and therefore also unread.

So strike a balance. If you judge that a group wishes to be known by a particular term, that the term is widely understood and that using any other would seem odd, old-fashioned or offensive, then use it. Context may be important: *Coloured* is a common term in South Africa for people of mixed race; it is not considered derogatory. Elsewhere it may be. Remember that both times and terms change: expressions that were in common use a few decades ago are now odious. Nothing is to be gained by casually insulting your readers.

But do not labour to avoid imaginary insults, especially if the effort does violence to the language. So avoid terms like *the non-disabled person* used (on BBC Radio 3) to mean *normal person.* Some people, such as the members of the Task-force on Bias-Free Language of the Association of American University Presses, believe that *ghetto-blaster* is "offensive as a stereotype of African-American culture", that it is invidious to speak of a *normal* child, that *massacre* should not be used "to refer to a successful American Indian raid or battle victory against white colonisers and invaders", and that the use of the term *cretin* is distressing. They want, they say, to avoid "victimisation" and to get "the person before the disability". The intent may be admirable, but they are unduly sensitive, often inventing slights where none exists. The term *cretin* came into use as a way of acknowledging the essential humanity of a physically deformed or intellectually subnormal person. It is now used for a definable medical condition. The aversion to *cretin* may arise from its slight similarity to *cripple*, a plain word now almost universally discarded in favour of the euphemistic *physically handicapped* or *disabled.*

Thomas Bowdler provides a cautionary example. His version of Shakespeare, produced in 1818 using "judicious" paraphrase and expurgation, was designed to be read by men to their families so that no one would be offended or embarrassed. In doing so, he gave his name to an insidious form of censorship (bowdlerism).

Some people believe the possibility of giving offence, causing embarrassment, lowering self-esteem, reinforcing stereotypes, perpetuating prejudice, victimising, marginalising or discriminating to be more important than stating the truth, never mind the chance of doing so with any verve or panache. They are wrong. Do not self-bowdlerise your prose. You may be neither Galileo nor Salman Rushdie, but you too may sometimes be right to cause offence. Your first duty is to the truth.

he, she, they You also have a duty to grammar. The struggle to be gender-neutral rests on a misconception about gender, a grammatical convention to make words masculine, feminine or neuter. Since English is unusual in assigning few genders to nouns other than those relating to people (ships are exceptions), feminists have come to argue that language should be gender-neutral.

This would be a forlorn undertaking in most tongues, and even in English it presents difficulties. It may be no tragedy that *policemen* are now almost always *police officers* and *firemen* *firefighters*, but to call *chairmen chairs* serves chiefly to remind everyone that the world of committees and those who make it go round are largely devoid of humour. Avoid also *chairpersons* (*chairwoman* is permissible but unnecessary), *humankind* and the *person in the street* – ugly expressions all.

119

It is no more demeaning to women to use the words *actress,
ballerina* or *seamstress* than *goddess, princess* or *queen.* (Similarly,
you should feel as free to separate *Siamese twins* or *welsh* on
debts – at your own risk – as you would to go on a *Dutch treat,*
pass through *french windows,* or play *Russian roulette.* Note,
though, that you risk being *dogged* by *catty* language police.)

If you believe it is "exclusionary" or insulting to women to
use *he* in a general sense, you can rephrase some sentences in
the plural. Thus *Instruct the reader without lecturing him* may be
put as *Instruct readers without lecturing them.* But some sentences
resist this treatment: *Find a good teacher and take his advice* is
not easily rendered gender-neutral. So do not be ashamed of
sometimes using *man* to include *women,* or making *he* do for
she.

And, so long as you are not insensitive in other ways, few
women will be offended if you restrain yourself from putting *or
she* after every *he.*

He or she which hath no stomach to this fight,
Let him or her depart; his or her passport shall be made,
And crowns for convoy put into his or her purse:
We would not die in that person's company
That fears his or her fellowship to die with us.
(Shakespeare, "Henry V")

In some contexts, though, *she* can be a substitute for *he*:
That ever was thrall, now is he free;
That ever was small, now great is she;
Now shall God deem both thee and me
Unto His bliss if we do well.
(15th-century carol)

The Oxford English Dictionary now accepts the use of "their"
in examples like the following, but note that they still involve a
nasty scrambling of syntax.

*We can't afford to squander anyone's talents, whatever colour their
skin is.*

*When someone takes their own life, they leave their loved ones with
an agonising legacy of guilt.*

There's a child somewhere in Birmingham and all across the country and needs somebody to put their arm around them and to say: "I love you; you're a part of America." (George Bush)

See also **ethnic groups, gender, tribe.**

populace is a term for the *common people*, not a synonym for the *population.*

positive means *definitely laid down, beyond possibility of doubt, absolute, fully convinced* or *greater than zero.* It does not mean *good. It was a positive meeting* probably means *It was a good,* or *fruitful, meeting.*

practical, practicable *Practical* means *useful; practicable* means *feasible.*

pre- is often unnecessary as a prefix, as in *pre-announced, precondition, pre-prepared, pre-cooked.* If it seems to be serving a function, try making use of a word such as already or earlier: *Here's one I cooked earlier.*

Pre-owned is *second-hand.*

premier (as a noun) should be confined to the first ministers of Canadian provinces, German *Länder* and other subnational states. Do not use it as a synonym for the prime minister of a country.

presently means *soon*, not *at present.* ("Presently Kep opened the door of the shed, and let out Jemima Puddle-Duck." Beatrix Potter)

press, pressure, pressurise *Pressurise* is what you want in an aircraft, but not in an argument or encounter where persuasion is being employed – the verb you want there is *press.* Use *pressure* only as a noun.

prevaricate, procrastinate *Prevaricate* means *evade the truth; procrastinate* means *delay.* ("Procrastination" – or punctuality, if you are Oscar Wilde – "is the thief of time.")

pristine means *original* or *former*; it does not mean *clean*.

proactive Not a pretty word: try *active* or *energetic*.

process Some writers see their prose in industrial terms: *education* becomes an *education process*, *elections* an *electoral process*, *development* a *development process*, *writing* a *writing process*. If you follow this fashion, do not be surprised if readers switch off.

prodigal If you are *prodigal*, that does not mean you are *welcomed home* or *taken back without recrimination*. It means you have *squandered your patrimony*.

proofreading *see* Part 3.

propaganda (which is singular) means a *systematic effort to spread doctrine or opinions*. It is not a synonym for *lies*.

protagonist means the *chief actor* or *combatant*. If you are referring to several people, they cannot all be protagonists.

protest By all means *protest your innocence*, or *your intention to write good English*, if you are making a declaration. But if you are making a complaint or objection, you must *protest at* or *against* it.

pry Unless you mean *peer* or *peep*, the word you probably should be using is *prise*.

public schools in Britain, the places where fee-paying parents send their children; in the United States, the places where they don't.

punctuation Some guidelines on common problems.

apostrophes

1   With singular words and names that end in *s* use the normal possessive ending *'s*:
    boss's
    caucus's

Delors's
Jones's
St James's
Shanks's

2 After plurals that do not end in s also use 's: *children's*,
Frenchmen's, *media's*.

3 Use the ending s' on plurals that end in s: *Danes'*, *bosses'*,
Joneses'.

And on plural names that take a singular verb:
Barclays'
Cisco Systems'
Reuters'

4 Some plural nouns, although singular in other respects, such
as the United States, the United Nations, the Philippines,
have a plural possessive apostrophe:
Who will be the United States' next president?

In general, however, try to avoid United States', Congress's,
and all such formations which are horrible to read silently,
and even worse aloud.

5 *Lloyd's* (the insurance market): try to avoid using as a
possessive; like Christie's and Sotheby's it poses an insoluble
problem.

6 *Achilles heel*: the vulnerable part of the hero of the Trojan
war.

7 Decades do not have apostrophes: *the 1990s*.

8 Phrases like *two weeks' time, four days' march, six months'
leave* need apostrophes. So do those involving *worth*, when it
follows a quantity or other measurement: *three months' worth
of imports, a manifesto's worth of insincerity* (*see also* **hyphens**,
page 75).

9 People:
people's = of (the) people
peoples' = of peoples
See also **grammar and syntax** (false possessive).

brackets If a whole sentence is within brackets, put the full stop inside. Square brackets should be used for interpolations in direct quotations: "*Let them [the poor] eat cake.*" To use ordinary brackets implies that the words inside them were part of the original text from which you are quoting.

colons Use a colon "to deliver the goods that have been invoiced in the preceding words" (Fowler).
They brought presents: gold, frankincense and oil at $100 a barrel.

Use a colon before a whole quoted sentence, but not before a quotation that begins in mid-sentence.
She said: "It will never work." He retorted that it had "always worked before".

commas Use commas as an aid to understanding. Too many in one sentence can be confusing.

1   It is not always necessary to put a comma after a short phrase at the start of a sentence if no natural pause exists:
That night she took a tumble.

2   But a breath, and so a comma, is needed after longer passages:
When day broke and she was able at last to see what had happened, she realised she had fallen through the roof and into the Big Brother house.

3   Use two commas, or none at all, when inserting a clause in the middle of a sentence. Thus, do not write:
Use two commas, or none at all when inserting ... or
Use two commas or none at all, when inserting ...

Similarly, two commas or none at all are needed with constructions like:
And, though he denies it, he couldn't tell a corncrake from a cornflake ...
But, when Bush came to Shuv, he found it wasn't a town, just a Hebrew word for Return.

4   American states: commas are usual after the names of American states when these are written as though they

were part of an address: *Kansas City, Kansas, proves that even Kansas City needn't always be Missourible* (Ogden Nash). But do not do so where it offends against grammar, as before "and", or where it produces too many commas for the sentence to stand. Apply your discretion.

5 For sense: commas can alter the sense of a sentence. To write *Mozart's 40th symphony, in G minor*, with commas indicates that this symphony was written in G minor. Without commas, *Mozart's 40th symphony in G minor* suggests he wrote 39 other symphonies in G minor.

6 Lists: do not put a comma before *and* at the end of a sequence of items unless one of the items includes another *and*. Thus:
The doctor suggested an aspirin, half a grapefruit and a cup of broth. But he ordered scrambled eggs, whisky and soda, and a selection from the trolley.

7 Question-marks: do not put commas after question-marks, even when they would be separated by inverted commas:
"May I have a second helping?" he asked.

8 Quotations: within a sentence a quotation needs to be preceded by a comma, or a colon, or a word such as *that* (or *if, because, whether* etc), if it is an entire sentence. The first quoted word should also have an initial capital. Thus *The doctor responded, "You'll probably be better in the morning, or dead," before sampling a crème caramel.* If the words quoted are not an entire sentence, neither comma nor capital is needed: *The doctor responded that he would "probably be better in the morning, or dead," before sampling a crème caramel.* In this example, it is known that the final quoted word was followed by a punctuation mark – a full stop, converted in the quotation into a comma – so the final comma is placed within the inverted commas. If, however, it is not known whether the quoted words constituted a full sentence, assume that the quotation is unpunctuated and put the appropriate punctuation mark outside the inverted commas: *Having impaled himself with a handle-bar in the*

back of the cab, he was heard to say he "now realised what was meant by fatal attraction".

If you want to quote a full sentence and precede it with the word *that* (etc), no comma is needed before the inverted commas, but the first quoted word still needs an initial capital: *On learning that he was only scratched, her comment was that "Next time I hope Cupid's dart will be tipped with curare."*

See also **inverted commas** *below.*

dashes You can use dashes in pairs for parenthesis, but not more than one pair per sentence, ideally not more than one pair per paragraph.

"Use a dash to introduce an explanation, amplification, paraphrase, particularisation or correction of what immediately precedes it. Use it to gather up the subject of a long sentence. Use it to introduce a paradoxical or whimsical ending to a sentence. Do not use it as a punctuation maid-of-all-work." (Gowers)

Do not use a parenthetical dash as a catch-all punctuation device when a comma, colon, etc could be used. The much-reviled semi-colon is often worth an airing, too.

full stops Use plenty. They keep sentences short. This helps the reader. Do not use full stops in abbreviations or at the end of headings and subheadings.

inverted commas (quotation marks) Use single ones only for quotations within quotations. Thus:
"When I say 'immediately', I mean some time before April," said the builder.

For the relative placing of quotation marks and punctuation, follow Oxford rules. Thus, if an extract ends with a full stop or question-mark, put the punctuation before the closing inverted commas.
His maxim was that "love follows laughter." In this spirit came his opening gambit: "What's the difference between a buffalo and a bison?"

If a complete sentence in quotes comes at the end of a larger sentence, the final stop should be inside the inverted commas. Thus:

The answer was, "You can't wash your hands in a buffalo." She replied, "Your jokes are execrable."

If the quotation does not include any punctuation, the closing inverted commas should precede any punctuation marks that the sentence requires. Thus:

She had already noticed that the "young man" looked about as young as the New Testament is new. Although he had been described as "fawnlike in his energy and playfulness", "a stripling with all the vigour and freshness of youth", and even as "every woman's dream toyboy", he struck his companion-to-be as the kind of old man warned of by her mother as "not safe in taxis". Where, now that she needed him, was "Mr Right"?

When a quotation is broken off and resumed after such words as *he said*, ask yourself whether it would naturally have had any punctuation at the point where it is broken off. If the answer is yes, a comma is placed within the quotation marks to represent this. Thus:

"If you'll let me see you home," he said, "I think I know where we can find a cab."

The comma after home belongs to the quotation and so comes within the inverted commas, as does the final full stop.

But if the words to be quoted are continuous, without punctuation at the point where they are broken, the comma should be outside the inverted commas. Thus:

"My bicycle", she assured him, "awaits me."

Do not use quotation marks unnecessarily:

Her admirer described his face as a "finely chiselled work of art"; she wrote in her diary that it looked more like a "collapsed lung".

Note that the Bible contains no quotation marks, with no consequent confusions.

question-marks Except in sentences that include a question in inverted commas, question-marks always come at the end of the sentence. Thus:

Where could he get a drink, he wondered?
Had Zimri peace, who slew his master?

semi-colons Use them to mark a pause longer than a comma and shorter than a full stop. Don't overdo them.

Use them to distinguish phrases listed after a colon only if commas will not do the job clearly. Thus:
They agreed on only three points: the ceasefire should be immediate; it should be internationally supervised, preferably by the AU; and a peace conference should be held, either in Geneva or in Ouagadougou.

question-marks *see* **punctuation**.

quite In America, *quite* is usually an intensifying adverb similar to *altogether*, *entirely* or *very*; in Britain, depending on the emphasis, the tone of voice and the adjective that follows, it usually means *fairly, moderately* or *reasonably*, and often damns with faint praise.

quotes Be sparing with quotes. Direct quotes should be used when either the speaker or what was said is surprising, or when the words used are particularly pithy or graphic. Otherwise you can probably paraphrase more concisely. The most pointless quote is the inconsequential remark attributed to a nameless source: *"Everyone wants to be in on the act," says one high-ranking civil servant.*

For *quotation marks* (inverted commas), *see* **punctuation**.

real Is it really necessary? When used to mean *after taking inflation into account*, it is legitimate. In other contexts (*Investors are showing real interest in the country, but Colombians wonder if real prosperity will ever arrive*) it is often better left out.

rebut, refute *Rebut* means *repel* or *meet in argument*. *Refute*, which is stronger, means *disprove*. Neither should be used as a synonym for *deny*. "Shakespeare never has six lines together without a fault. Perhaps you may find seven: but this does not refute my general assertion." (Samuel Johnson)

red and blue In Britain, colours that are associated with socialism and conservatism respectively; in the United States, colours that are associated with Republicans and Democrats respectively. They are very confusing to the large number of readers who associate red with the political left, and should therefore be avoided, especially in the American context.

redact in Latin means *bring back*. It is now also used to mean *obscure, blot out, obliterate*, as when testimony thought harmful to national security is officially blacked out in documents. Use it only in that narrowly technical sense.

redolent means *smelling of, fragrant*. Do not therefore write *redolent of the smell of linseed oil and turpentine*.

reduce, diminish, lessen, shrink are not interchangeable. *Reduce* is transitive, so must be followed by a noun. *Diminish* and *shrink* can be transitive or intransitive. So can *lessen*, though it is usually used before a noun.

redux A word often dropped into headlines by pretentious people anxious to impress. It is seldom clear what they mean. Avoid.

references *see* **footnotes, sources, references** in Part 3.

regrettably means *to be regretted*. Do not confuse with *regretfully*, used of someone showing regret.

relationship is a long word often better replaced by *relations*. *The two countries hope for a better relationship* means *The two countries hope for better relations*. But *relationship* is an appropriate word for two people in a close friendship.

report on not *into*.

Republican A long word, but not so long that it needs replacing with *red* (see above), or *GOP* (*for* Grand Old Party), which is as meaningless as *red* to non-American readers.

reshuffle, resupply *Shuffle* and *supply* will do, except for British Cabinets, which are *reshuffled* from time to time.

resources, resourceful *Resourceful* is a useful word; the term *natural resources*, less satisfactory, also has its merits. Most other uses of *resource* tend to be vile. The word is entirely at home in the following sentence, taken from an advertisement placed by Skill for Business (2005): "Sector Skills Councils ... assess what resource is already out there, and then create comprehensive deals with supply-side partners to fill skills gaps and shortages." Beware.

revert means *return to* or *go back to*, as in *The garden has reverted to wilderness*. It does not mean *come back to* or *get back to*, as in *I'll give you an answer as soon as I can*.

Richter scale Beloved of journalists, the Richter scale is unknown to seismologists. The strength of an earthquake is its *magnitude*, so say *an earthquake of magnitude 8.9*. See **earthquakes** in Part 3.

ring, wring (verbs) bells are rung; hands are wrung. Both may be seen at weddings.

Roma is the name of the people. Their language is *Romany*. Remember that *Sinti* are also Gypsies.

run In countries with a presidential system you may *run* for office. In those with a parliamentary one, you *stand*.

Russian names *see* **names.**

S

same is often superfluous. If your sentence contains *on the same day that*, try *on the day that*.

scotch To *scotch* means to *disable*, not to *destroy*. ("*We have scotched the snake, not killed it.*" "Macbeth") The people may also be *Scotch, Scots* or *Scottish*; choose as you like. *Scot-free* means completely free from payment of a fine (or punishment), not *free from Scotsmen*.

second-biggest (third-oldest, fourth-wisest, fifth-commonest, etc) Think before you write.
Apart from New York, a Bramley is the second-biggest apple in the world. Other than home-making and parenting, prostitution is the third-oldest profession. After Tom, Dick and Harriet, Henry I was the fourth-wisest fool in Christendom. Besides justice, prudence, temperance and fortitude, the fifth-commonest virtue of the Goths was punctuality.

None of these sentences should contain the ordinal (second- , third- , fourth- , fifth- , etc).

sector Try *industry* instead or, for example, *banks* instead of *banking sector*.

semi-colons *see* **punctuation**.

sensual, sensuous *Sensual* means *carnal* or *voluptuous. Sensuous* means *pertaining to aesthetic appreciation*, without any implication of lasciviousness.

sequestered, sequestrated *Sequestered* means *secluded*. *Sequestrated* means *confiscated* or *made bankrupt*.

short words Use them. They are often Anglo-Saxon rather than Latin in origin. They are easy to spell and easy to understand. Thus prefer:

about *to* approximately	plant *to* facility
after *to* following	set up *to* establish
before *to* prior to	show *to* demonstrate
but *to* however	spending *to* expenditure
enough *to* sufficient	take part *to* participate
let *to* permit	use *to* utilise
make *to* manufacture	

Underdeveloped countries are often better described as *poor*. *Substantive* often means *real* or *big*. "Short words are best and the old words when short are best of all." (Winston Churchill)

shrug This means to draw up the shoulders, so do not write *She shrugged her shoulders*.

simplistic Prefer *simple-minded, naive*.

Singaporean names *see* **names.**

singular or plural? *see* **grammar and syntax.**

skills are turning up all over the place – in learning skills, thinking skills, teaching skills – instead of *the ability to. He has the skills* probably means *He can.*

skyrocketed *Rocketed*, not *skyrocketed*.

slither, sliver As a noun, *slither* is *scree*. As a verb, it means *slide*. If you mean a *slice*, the word you want is *sliver*.

sloppy writing Use words with care.
If *This door is alarmed*, does its hair stand on end? If this envelope says *Urgent: dated material*, is it really too old-fashioned to be worth reading? Is a *handicapped toilet* really *faultily*

designed or *carrying extra weight*? Is *offensive marketing* just rude salesmanship?

More serious difficulties may arise with *indicted war criminals*. As their lawyers could one day remind you, these may turn out to be *innocent people accused of war crimes*.

Some familiar words may cause trouble. When Gordon Brown wrote in the *Guardian*, "No one can *underestimate* the scale of the challenge climate change represents," he presumably meant just the opposite. A *heart condition* is usually a *bad heart*. A *near miss* is probably a *near hit*. *Positive thoughts* (held by long-suffering creditors, according to *The Economist*) presumably means *optimism*, just as a *negative* report is probably a *critical* report. *Industrial action* is usually *industrial inaction, industrial disruption* or a *strike*. A *courtesy call* is generally a *sales offer* or an *uninvited visit*. A *substantially finished* bridge is an *unfinished* bridge. Someone with *high name-recognition* is *well known*. Something with *reliability problems* probably *does not work*. If yours is a *live audience*, what would a dead one be like?

And what is an *ethics violation*? An error of judgment? A crime? A moral lapse?

See also **unnecessary words**.

small capitals *see* **abbreviations** (small caps usage).

smart used to mean only *well dressed*, but *smart cards, smart sanctions* and *smart weapons*, etc are now universally with us, to the point where you may have to find another word (*elegant, chic, natty*) for *well-dressed*. *Smartly* still seems to work as an adverb suggesting prompt efficiency.

social security in America, *Social Security* means *pensions* and should be capitalised. Elsewhere it usually means *state benefits* more generally, which are called *welfare* in the United States.

soft is an adverb as well as an adjective and a noun. *Softly* is also an adverb. You can speak softly and carry a big stick, but if you have a quiet voice you are *soft* – not *softly* – *spoken*.

soi-disant means *self-styled*, not *so-called*.

sources *see* **footnotes, sources, references** in Part 3.

Spanish names *see* **names.**

specific A *specific* is a *medicine*, not a *detail*.

spelling Use British English rather than American English or any other kind. Sometimes, however, this injunction will clash with the rule that people and companies should be called what they want to be called, short of festooning themselves with titles. If it does, adopt American (or Canadian or other local) spelling when it is used in the name of an American (etc) company or private organisation (*Alcan Aluminum, Carter Center, Pulverizing Services Inc, Travelers Insurance*), but not when it is used for a government institution or a think-tank (*Department of Defence, Department of Labour, Pew Centre for Research*). The principle behind this ruling is that placenames are habitually changed from foreign languages into English: *Deutschland* becomes *Germany, München Munich, Torino Turin*, etc. And to respect the local spelling of government institutions would present difficulties: a sentence containing both the *Department of Labor* and the *secretary of labour*, or the *Defense Department* and the *need for a strong defence*, would look unduly odd. That oddity will arise nonetheless if you have to explain that *Rockefeller Center Properties is in charge of Rockefeller Centre*, but with luck that will not happen too often. *See* **placenames.**

    The Australian *Labor Party* should be spelt without a *u* not only because it is not a government institution but also because the Australians spell it that way, even though they spell *labour* as the British do.

s spelling Use -*ise*, -*isation* (*realise, organisation*) throughout. But please do not *hospitalise*.

common problems

abattoir	accommodate
abut, abutted, abutting	acknowledgment

acquittal, acquitted, acquitting
adrenalin
adviser, advisory
aeon
aeroplane
aesthetic
aficionado
Afrikaans (the language),
  Afrikaner (the person)
ageing (*but* caging, paging,
  raging, waging)
agri-business (*not* agro-
  business)
aircraft, airliner
algorithm
al-Qaeda
amiable
amid (*not* amidst)
amok (*not* amuck)
among (*not* amongst)
annex (verb), annexe
  (noun)
antecedent
appal, appals, appalling,
  appalled
aqueduct
aquifer
arbitrager
artefact
asinine
balk (*not* baulk)
balloted, balloting
bandanna
bandwagon
battalion
bellwether
benefiting, benefited
biased

bicentenary (noun, *not*
  bicentennial)
billeting, billeted
blanketing, blanketed
block (*never* bloc)
blowzy (*not* blousy)
bogey (bogie is on a
  locomotive)
borsch
braggadocio
brethren
bumf
bused, busing (keep bussing
  for kissing)
by-election, bylaw, bypass,
  by-product, byword
bye (in sport)
caddie (golf), caddy (tea)
caesium
cannon (gun), canon
  (standard, criterion,
  clergyman)
cappuccino
carcass
caviar
chancy
channelling, channelled
checking account (spell it
  thus when explaining
  to Americans a current
  account, which is to be
  preferred)
choosy
cipher
clubable (coined, and
  spelled thus, by Dr
  Johnson)
colour, colouring, colourist

combating, combated
commemorate
connection
consensus
cooled, cooler, coolly
coral (stuff found in sea),
    corral (cattle pen)
coruscate
cosseted, cosseting
defendant
dependant (person),
    dependent (adj)
depository (unless referring
    to American depositary
    receipts)
desiccate, desiccation
detente (*not* détente)
dexterous (*not* dextrous)
dignitary
dilapidate
disk (in a computer context),
    otherwise disc (including
    compact disc)
dispatch (*not* despatch)
dispel, dispelling
distil, distiller
divergences
doppelganger(s)
doveish
dryer, dryly
dullness
dwelt
dyeing (colour)
dyke
ecstasy
embarrass (*but* harass)
encyclopedia
enroll, enrolment

ensure (make certain), insure
    (against risks)
enthrall
extrovert
farther (distance), further
    (additional)
favour, favourable
ferreted
fetus (*not* foetus,
    misformed from the Latin
    fetus)
field-marshal (soldier)
Filipino, Filipina (person),
    Philippine (adj of the
    Philippines)
filleting, filleted
flotation
flyer, frequent flyer, high-flyer
focused, focusing
forbear (abstain), forebear
    (ancestor)
forbid, forbade
foreboding
foreclose
forefather
forestall
forewarn
forgather
forgo (do without), forego
    (precede)
forsake
forswear, forsworn
fuelled
-ful, not -full (thus armful,
    bathful, handful, etc)
fulfil, fulfilling
fullness
fulsome

funnelling, funnelled
furore
gallivant
gelatine
glamour, glamorise,
   glamorous
graffito, graffiti
gram (*not* gramme)
grey
guerrilla
gulag
Gurkha
gypsy
haj
hallo (*not* hello)
harass (*but* embarrass)
hiccup (*not* hiccough)
high-tech
Hizbullah
honour, honourable
hotch-potch
humour, humorist, humorous
hurrah (*not* hooray)
idiosyncrasy
impostor
impresario
inadvertent
incur, incurring
innocuous
inoculate
inquire, inquiry (*not* enquire,
   enquiry)
install, instalment, installation
instil, instilling
intransigent
jail (not gaol)
Janjaweed
jewellery (*not* jewelry)

judgment
kilogram or kilo (*not*
   kilogramme)
labelling, labelled
laissez-faire
lama (priest), llama (beast)
lambast (*not* lambaste)
launderette
leukaemia
levelled
libelling, libelled
licence (noun), license (verb),
   licensee (person with a
   licence)
limited
linchpin, lynch law
liquefy
literal
littoral (shore)
logarithm
loth (reluctant), loathe (hate),
   loathsome
low-tech
madrassa
manilla envelope, *but* Manila,
   capital of the Philippines
manoeuvre, manoeuvring
marshal (noun and verb),
   marshalled
mayonnaise
medieval
mêlée
meter (a measuring tool),
   metre (metric measure,
   meter in American)
mileage
millennium, but
   millenarian

139

minuscule
moccasin
modelling, modelled
mould
Muslim (*not* Moslem)
naivety
'Ndrangheta
nonplussed
nought (for numerals),
    otherwise naught
obbligato
occur, occurring
oesophagus
oestrus (oestrogen, etc)
optics (optician,
    etc) ophthalmic
    (ophthalmology, etc)
paediatric, paediatrician
palaeontology,
    palaeontologist
panel, panelled
paraffin
parallel, paralleled
pastime
pavilion
phoney (*not* phony)
piggyback (*not* pickaback)
plummeted, plummeting
poky
practice (noun), practise
    (verb)
praesidium (*not* presidium)
predilection
preferred (preferring, *but*
    proffered)
preventive (*not* preventative)
pricey
primeval

principal (head, loan; or adj),
    principle (abstract noun)
proffered (proffering, *but*
    preferred)
profited
program (only in a computer
    context), otherwise
    programme
prophecy (noun), prophesy
    (verb)
protester
Pushtu (language), Pushtun
    (people)
pygmy
pzazz
queuing
rack, racked, racking (as in
    racked with pain, nerve-
    racking)
racket
rankle
rarefy
razzmatazz
recur, recurrent, recurring
regretted, regretting
restaurateur
resuscitate
rhythm
rivet (riveted, riveter,
    riveting)
rococo
ropy
rottweiler
rumoured
sacrilegious
sanatorium
savannah
seize

shaky

sharia

shenanigans

sheriff

Shia (noun and adj), Shias, Shiism

shibboleth

Sibylline

siege

sieve

siphon (*not* syphon)

skulduggery

smelt

smidgen (*not* smidgeon)

smoky

smooth (both noun and verb)

snigger (*not* snicker)

sobriquet

somersault

soothe

souped up

soyabean

specialty (only in context of medicine, steel and chemicals), otherwise speciality

sphinx

spoilt

squirrelled

stanch (verb)

staunch (adj)

storey (floor)

straitjacket and strait-laced *but* straight-faced

stratagem

strategy

Sunni, Sunnis

supersede

swap (not swop)

swathe

synonym

Taliban (plural)

taoiseach (*but* prefer prime minister, or leader)

tariff

Tatar (*not* Tartar)

threshold

titbits

titillate

tonton-macoutes

tormentor

trade union, trade unions (*but* Trades Union Congress)

transatlantic, transpacific

transferred, transferring

travelled

tricolor

trouper (as in old trouper)

tsar

tyre

unnecessary

unparalleled

untrammelled

vaccinate

vacillate

vermilion

wacky

wagon (*not* waggon)

weasel, weaselly

while *not* whilst

wiggle (*not* wriggle) room

wilful

wisteria

withhold

yarmulke (prefer to *kippah*)

yogurt

-able

debatable	indictable	tradable
dispensable	indispensable	unmissable
disputable	indistinguishable	unmistakable
forgivable	lovable	unshakable
imaginable	movable	unusable
implacable	ratable	usable
indescribable	salable (but prefer sellable)	

-eable

bridgeable	manageable	unenforceable
changeable	noticeable	unpronounceable
knowledgeable	serviceable	sizeable
likeable	traceable	

-ible

accessible	feasible	irresistible
convertible	inadmissible	permissible
digestible	indestructible	submersible
dismissible	investible	

plurals No rules here. The spelling of the following plurals may have been decided by either practice or derivation.

-a

consortia	memoranda	sanatoria
corrigenda	millennia	spectra
data	phenomena	strata
media	quanta	

-ae

alumnae (female)	antennae
amoebae	formulae

-eaus

bureaus	plateaus

-eaux

chateaux	tableaux

-fs, -efs

dwarfs	roofs
oafs	still-lifes

-i

alumni	nuclei	termini
bacilli	stimuli	

-oes

archipelagoes	haloes	potatoes
buffaloes	heroes	salvoes
cargoes	innuendoes	tomatoes
desperadoes	mangoes	tornadoes
dominoes	mementoes	torpedoes
echoes	mosquitoes	vetoes
embargoes	mottoes	volcanoes
frescoes	noes	

-os

albinos	flamingos	provisos
armadillos	folios	quangos
calicos	ghettos	radios
casinos	impresarios	silos
commandos	librettos	solos
demos	manifestos	sopranos
dynamos	memos	stilettos
egos	mulattos	studios
embryos	neutrinos	virtuosos
Eskimos	oratorios	weirdos
falsettos	peccadillos	zeros
fandangos	pianos	
fiascos	placebos	

-s

agendas

-ums

conundrums	moratoriums	referendums
crematoriums	nostrums	stadiums
curriculums	premiums	symposiums
forums	quorums	ultimatums

-uses

buses	fetuses	prospectuses
caucuses	focuses	syllabuses
circuses	geniuses	

-ves

calves	loaves	wharves
halves	scarves	
hooves	turves	

Note: *indexes* (of books), but *indices* (indicators, index numbers); *appendices* (supplements), but *appendixes* (anatomical organs).

split infinitives see **grammar and syntax**.

stanch, staunch *Stanch* the flow, though the man be *staunch* (*loyal, stout-hearted*). The distinction is useful, if bogus (since both words derive from the same old-French *estancher*).

stationary, stationery *Stationary* is still; *stationery* is writing paper, envelopes, etc.

stentorian, stertorous *Stentorian* means *loud* (like the voice of Stentor, a warrior in the Trojan war). *Stertorous* means *characterised by a snoring sound* (from *sterto*, snore).

straight, strait *Straight* means *direct* or *uncurved*; *strait* means *narrow* or *tight*. The *strait-laced* tend to be *straight-faced*. *Straits* are narrow bodies of water between bits of land.

strategy, strategic *Strategy* may sometimes have some merit, especially in military contexts, as a contrast to *tactics*. But *strategic* is usually meaningless except to tell you that the writer is pompous and is trying to invest something with a seriousness it does not deserve.

-style Avoid *German-style supervisory boards, an* EU-*style rotating presidency*, etc. Explain what you mean.

subcontract If you engage someone to do something, you are *contracting* the job to that person (or company); only if that person (or company) then asks someone else to do it is the job *subcontracted.*

surreal Surrealism was a revolutionary movement of philosophers, writers and artists who in the 1920s wanted to change the world by drawing on the subconscious, escaping the control of reason and bringing about "the state where the distinction between the subjective and the objective loses its necessity and value" (André Breton). Occasionally *surreal* is used in reference to this movement. More often it is used freely to describe anything bizarre or peculiar, as in the paintings of Salvador Dali or René Magritte. Avoid casually debasing the word.

swear words Avoid them, unless they convey something genuinely helpful or interesting to the reader (eg, you are quoting someone). Usually, they will annoy rather than shock. But if you do use them, spell them out in full, without asterisks.

Swiss names *see* **names.**

syntax *see* **grammar and syntax.**

systemic, systematic *Systemic* means *relating to a system or body as a whole. Systematic* means *according to system, methodical* or *intentional.*

table Avoid *table* as a transitive verb. In Britain to *table* means to bring something forward for action, and should be kept to committees. In America it sometimes means exactly the opposite.

target Not so long ago *target* was almost unknown as a verb, except when used to mean *provide with a shield*. Now it turns up everywhere, even though *aim* or *direct* would often serve as well.

terrorist Use with care, preferably only to mean *someone who uses terror as an organised system of intimidation*. Prefer suspected terrorists to terrorist suspects.

testament, testimony A *testament* is a will; *testimony* is evidence. It is *testimony to the poor teaching of English that journalists habitually write testament instead*.

the Occasionally, the use of the definite article may be optional: *Maximilien Robespierre, the leader of the Committee of Public Safety*, is preferable to *Maximilien Robespierre, leader of the Committee of Public Safety*, but in this context the *the* after *Robespierre* is not essential. However, *Given that leaders of mainstream left and right parties* means something different from *Given that the leaders of both mainstream left and right parties*. Likewise, *If polls are right* means something different from *If the polls are right*. *They include freedom to set low flat taxes* is similarly, if subtly, different from *They include the freedom to set low flat taxes*. In each of these examples the crucial *the* was left out. *See also* **grammar and syntax**.

there is, there are Often unnecessary. *There are three problems facing the prime minister* is better as *Three problems face the prime minister*.

throe, throw *Throe* is a *spasm* or *pang* (and is usually in the plural). *Throw* is to *cast* or *hurl through the air*. *Last throws* may be all right on the cricket pitch, but *last throes* are more likely on the battlefield.

ticket, platform, manifesto The *ticket* lists the names of the candidates for a particular party (so if you *split your ticket* you vote for, eg, a Republican for president and a Democrat for Congress). The *platform* is the statement of basic principles (*planks*) put forward by an American party, usually at its pre-election convention. It is thus akin to a British party's *manifesto*, which sets out the party's policies.

time If you have to give an exact time, you should write 6.25*am*, 11.15*pm*, etc. But it is permissible to write *two o'clock, 11 o'clock, half past ten,* a *quarter past four*, if you wish to be less precise.

times Take care. *Three times more than X* is *four times as much as X*.

titles The overriding principle is to treat people with respect. That usually means giving them the title they themselves adopt. But some titles are ugly (Ms), some misleading (all Italian graduates are Dr) and some tiresomely long (Mr Dr Dr Federal Sanitary-Inspector Schmidt). Do not therefore indulge people's self-importance unless it would seem insulting not to.

Do not use Mr, Mrs, Miss, Ms or Dr on first mention. Plain *Barack Obama, David Beckham* or other appropriate combination of first name and surname will do. But thereafter the names of all living people should be preceded by Mr, Mrs, Miss or some other title. Serving soldiers, sailors, airmen, etc should be given their title on first and subsequent mentions. Those (such as Colin Powell, but not Pervez Musharraf) who cast aside their uniforms for civvy street become plain Mr (or whatever). Governor X, President Y, the Rev John Z may be Mr, Mrs or Miss on second mention.

On first mention use forename and surname; then drop the forename (unless there are two people with the same surname mentioned):
Nicolas Sarkozy, then *Mr Sarkozy*

1   Avoid nicknames and diminutives unless the person is always known (or prefers to be known) by one:
    Joe Biden Tony Blair Bill Emmott Maggie Smith Tiger Woods

2   Avoid the habit of joining office and name: *Prime Minister Brown, Enlargement Commissioner Olli Rehn.* But *Chancellor Merkel* is permissible.

3   Knights, dames, princes, kings, etc should have their titles on first and subsequent mentions. Many peers are, however, better known by their former names and can be given those on first mention. After that, they should be called by their titles. Life peeresses may be called *Lady*, not *Baroness*, just as barons are called *Lord.* Note that some people choose not to use their titles. So *Sir Donald Tsang*, for instance, prefers to be just *Mr Tsang.* (*See* British titles *below.*)

4   If you use a title, get it right. *Rear-Admiral* Jones should not, at least on first mention, be called *Admiral* Jones.

5   Titles are not necessary in headings or captions, although surnames are: no *Baracks, Davids, Gordons, Hillarys,* etc. Sometimes they can also be dispensed with for athletes and pop stars, if titles would make them seem more ridiculous than dignified.

6   The dead: no titles (including *Mr*, etc), except those whom you are writing about because they have just died. *Dr Johnson* and *Mr Gladstone* are also permissible. There is no need to use first names for well-known people such as *Einstein* or *Keats*, though you might choose to do so for people whose second names are more common, like *Inigo Jones.*

7   *Ms* is permissible, though avoid it if you can. To call a woman *Miss* is not to imply that she is unmarried, merely

that she goes by her maiden name. Married women who are known by their maiden names – eg, Aung San Suu Kyi, Jane Fonda – are therefore Miss, unless they have made it clear that they want to be called something else.

8   Foreign titles: take extra care.

9   Dr: use *Dr* only for qualified medical people, unless the correct alternative is not known or it would seem perverse to use *Mr*. And try to keep *Professor* for those who hold chairs, not just a university job or an inflated ego.

10 Middle initials: omit except in cases where confusion would be caused otherwise. George W. Bush is allowed; but nobody will imagine that the *Lyndon Johnson* you are writing about is *Lyndon A. Johnson* or *Lyndon C. Johnson*.

11 Some titles serve as names, and therefore have initial capitals, though are also descriptions: *the Archbishop of Canterbury*, *the Emir of Kuwait*. If you want to describe the office rather than the individual, use lower case: *The next archbishop of Canterbury will be a woman*. Use lower case in references simply to the *archbishop*, *the emir*: *The Duchess of Scunthorpe was in her finery, but the duke wore jeans*.

British titles Long incomprehensible to all foreigners and most Britons, British titles and forms of address now seem just as confusing to those who hold them. Snobbery, embarrassment and obscurity make it difficult to know whether to write Mrs Thatcher, Mrs Margaret Thatcher, Lady Thatcher, Baroness Thatcher, Lady Margaret Thatcher or Baroness Margaret Thatcher. Properly, she was Margaret, Baroness Thatcher, but on first mention the following are preferable: *Margaret Thatcher* or *Lady Thatcher*. On subsequent mentions, *Lady Thatcher* is fine. If the context is historical, *Margaret Thatcher* and thereafter *Mrs (now Lady) Thatcher*.

On first mention all *viscounts, earls, marquesses, dukes* should be given their titles (shorn of all Right Honourables, etc). Thereafter they can be plain *Lord* (except for dukes). *Barons*, a category that includes all *life peers*, can always be called *Lord*. The full names of *knights* should be spelled out on first mention. Thereafter they become *Sir Firstnameonly*.

clerical titles Ordained clerics should be given their proper titles on first and subsequent mentions, though not their full honorifics (no need for His Holiness, His Eminence, the Right Reverend, etc). But:
the Rev Michael Wall (thereafter Mr Wall)
Father Ted (Father Ted)
Bishop Cuthbert Auckland (Bishop Auckland)
Archbishop Desmond Tutu (Archbishop Tutu)

Imams, muftis, ayatollahs, rabbis, gurus, etc should be given an appropriate title if they use one, and it should be repeated on second and subsequent mentions, so:
Ayatollah Hossein-Ali Montazeri (Ayatollah Montazeri)
Rabbi Lionel Bloom (Rabbi Bloom)
Sri Sri Ravi Shankar (Sri Sri Ravi Shankar)

to or and? *To try and end the killing* does not mean the same as *to try to end the killing*.

tortuous, torturous *Tortuous* means *winding* or *twisting*. *Torturous* means *causing torture*.

total is all right as a noun, but as a verb prefer *amount to* or *add up to*.

transitive and intransitive verbs The distinction between transitive and intransitive verbs is often now disregarded, to the distress of those brought up to respect it. Transitive verbs require a direct object; intransitive do not. Many verbs are both transitive and intransitive, and some ditransitive, meaning they appear to govern two objects, one direct and one indirect (as in *She gave her husband a piece of her mind*).

But not all. Commit is transitive. By *committing yourself to the wrong person*, you would be committing a mistake, but at least it would be grammatical. Deplete, too, is transitive: stocks do not deplete, they are depleted. Deliver also requires an object, which is implicit in commands like *"Stand and deliver!"* and questions like *"Do you deliver?"* Reduce is also transitive. If you want to use it intransitively, try diminish. Halve is another verb that needs an object: do not write *The growth rate has halved* (rather it has fallen by half). And do not obsess.

Many intransitive verbs need to be followed by a preposition, either explicitly or implicitly. Agree is one such. If some*thing* is involved, you must agree to, on or about it. If some*body* is involved, you may agree with him, or perhaps agree to do something. Similarly, you may appeal against this injunction, but you may not appeal it. Nor may you cascade it to your colleagues, collapse it, though it may collapse of its own accord, still less migrate it or pause it. Do not progress it, either, if by that you mean advance it. Progress is also intransitive. And if you live in a pleasant city, do not call it liveable. Life may be liveable there, and life is for living; but cities are lived in, not lived.

Embark and disembark are both transitive and intransitive. But take care if you use them transitively: you may disembark people or goods from a ship or aircraft, but you may not disembark the ship or aircraft on which they have travelled.

In the past the intransitive use of present was seldom used except in obstetrics. Now symptoms present intransitively in every surgery, and other things elsewhere too. All such manifestations are unpleasant.

Even in the age of presentations, keep present transitive.

See **warn**.

transpire means *exhale*, not *happen*, *occur* or *turn out*.

transportation in America, a means of getting from A to B; in Britain, a means of getting rid of convicts.

tribe Regarded as politically incorrect in some circles, *tribe* is widely used in Africa and other places. It should not be regarded as derogatory and is often preferable to *ethnic group*. *See also* **ethnic groups, political correctness**.

trillion A thousand billion (*see* **figures**).

trooper, trouper An old trooper is an old *cavalry soldier* (supposedly good at swearing), old *private soldier* in a tank regiment, or old *mounted policeman*. An old trouper is an old *member of a theatrical company*, or perhaps a *good sort*.

Turk, Turkic, Turkmen, Turkoman, etc *see* **placenames**.

twinkle, twinkling *In the twinkling of an eye* means *in a very short time. Before he was even a twinkle in his father's eye* means *Before* (perhaps *just before*) *he was conceived.* So, more loosely, *Before the Model T was even a twinkle in Henry Ford's eye* could mean *Before Henry Ford was even thinking about a mass-produced car. Before the internet was even a twinkle in Al Gore's eyes,* however, suggests *Al Gore invented the internet.*

Ukrainian names *see* **names.**

underprivileged Since a privilege is a special favour or advantage, it is by definition not something to which everyone is entitled. So *underprivileged*, by implying the right to privileges for all, is not just ugly jargon but also nonsense.

unique do not use it unless it is true. Unique means, literally, of which there is only one.

unlike should not be followed by *in*. Like *like*, *unlike* governs nouns and pronouns, not verbs and clauses.

unnecessary words Some words add nothing but length to your prose. Use adjectives to make your meaning more precise and be cautious of those you find yourself using to make it more emphatic. The word *very* is a case in point. If it occurs in a sentence you have written, try leaving it out and see whether the meaning is changed. *The omens were good* may have more force than *The omens were very good*.

Avoid:
cutbacks (cuts will do)
large-scale (big)
the policymaking process (policymaking)
sale events (sales)
strike action (strike)
track record (record)
weather conditions (weather)
wilderness area (usually either a wilderness or a wild area)

This time around means *This time*, just as *any time soon* means *soon*. *On a daily/weekly/monthly basis* means *daily/weekly/ monthly*. And *at this moment in time* means *now* or *at present*. *Currently, actually* and *really* often serve no purpose.

Shoot off, or rather shoot, as many prepositions after verbs as possible. Thus:
Companies can be *bought* and *sold* rather than *bought up* and *sold off*.
Budgets may be *cut* rather than *cut back*.
Plots can be *hatched* but not *hatched up*.
Markets should be *freed*, rather than *freed up*.
Organisations should be *headed by* rather than *headed up by* chairmen.
People can *meet* rather than *meet with* each other.
Children can be *sent* to bed rather than *sent off* to bed – though if they are to *sit up* they must first *sit down*.
Pre-prepared just means *prepared*.
This advice you are given *free*, or *for nothing*, but not *for free*.

Certain words are often redundant:
The leader of the *so-called* Front for a Free Freedonia is the leader of the Front for a Free Freedonia.
A *top politician* or *top priority* is usually just a *politician* and certainly only a *priority*.
A *major speech* is usually just a *speech*, an *executive summary* a *summary* and a *role model* a *model*.
A *safe haven* is a *haven*, a *free gift* a *gift* and a *whole raft* a *raft* (who has ever had *half a raft*?).
Most probably and *most especially* are *probably* and *especially*.
the fact that can often be shortened to *that* (*That I did not do so was a self-indulgence*).
Loans to the *industrial and agricultural sectors* are just *loans to industry and farming*.
Member states or *member countries* of the EU may simply be referred to as *members*.

In general, be concise. Try to be economical in your account or argument ("*The best way to be boring is to leave nothing out*" – Voltaire). Similarly, try to be economical with words – but not with the truth. "*As a general rule, run your pen through every other word you have written; you have no idea what vigour it will give to your style*" (Sydney Smith). Raymond Mortimer put it even more crisply when commenting about Susan Sontag: "*Her journalism, like a diamond, will sparkle more if it is cut.*"

See *also* **community, jargon, sloppy writing.**

use and abuse are much used and abused. You *take* drugs, not *use* them (Does he use sugar?). And *drug abuse* is just *drug taking,* as is *substance abuse,* unless it is *glue sniffing* or *bun throwing.*

venerable means *worthy of reverence*. It is not a synonym for *old*.

venues Avoid them. Try *places*.

verbal Every agreement, except the nod-and-wink variety, is *verbal*. If you mean one that was not written down, describe it as *oral*.

viable means *capable of living*. Do not apply it to things like railway lines. *Economically viable* means *profitable*.

Vietnamese names *see* **names**.

wars Prefer lower case for the names of wars:
American civil war
cold war
Gulf war
war of the Spanish succession
the war of Jenkins' ear

But these are exceptions:
the Thirty Years War
the War of Independence
the Wars of the Roses

Write:
the first world war or *the 1914–18 war*, not *world war one*, I or 1
the second world war or *the 1939–45 war*, not *world war two*, II or 2

Post-war and *pre-war* are hyphenated.

which and that *Which* informs, *that* defines. *This is the house that Jack built.* But *This house, which Jack built, is now falling down.* Americans tend to be fussy about making a distinction between *which* and *that*. Good writers of British English are less fastidious. ("*We have left undone those things which we ought to have done.*")

while is best used temporally. Do not use it in place of *although* or *whereas*.

who, whom *Who* is one of the few words in English that differ in the accusative (objective) case, when it becomes *whom*, often throwing native English-speakers into a fizzle.

In the sentence *This is the man who can win the support of most Tory MPs*, the word you want is *who*, since *who* is the subject of the relative clause. It remains the subject, and therefore also *who*, in the sentence *This is the man who she believes (or says or insists, etc) can win the support of most Tory MPs*. That becomes clearer if the sentence is punctuated thus: *This is the man who, she believes (or says or insists, etc), can win the support of most Tory MPs*.

However, in the sentence *This is the man whom most Tory MPs can support*, the word in question is *whom* because the subject of the relative clause has become *most Tory MPs*. *Whom* is also necessary in the sentence *This is the man whom she believes to be able to win the support of most Tory MPs*. This is because the verb *believe* is here being used as a transitive verb, when it must be followed by an infinitive. If, however, the word *insists* were used instead of *believes*, the sentence could not be similarly changed, because the verb *insist* cannot be used transitively.

wrack is an old word meaning *vengeance, punishment* or *wreckage* (as in *wrack and ruin*). It can also be *seaweed*. And as a verb it can mean to *wreck, devastate* or *ruin*. It has nothing to do with *wreak*, and it is not an instrument of torture or a receptacle for toast: that is *rack*. Hence *racked with pain, by war, drought*, etc. *Rack* your brains – unless they be *wracked*.

part 2

American and British English

The differences between English as written and spoken in America and English as used in Britain are considerable, as is the potential for misunderstanding, even offence, when using words or phrases that are unfamiliar or that mean something else on the other side of the Atlantic. This section highlights the important differences between American and British English syntax and punctuation, spelling and usage. (There are also differences between American and Canadian English, but these are not covered here.)

A number of subjects call for detailed, specialised guidance beyond the scope of this book, though some of the vocabulary is dealt with here. These include food and cookery (different names for ingredients and equipment, different systems of measurement); medicine and health care (different professional titles, drug names, therapies); human anatomy; and gardening (different seasons and plants). Many crafts and hobbies also use different terms for equipment, materials and techniques. *See also* **Americanisms** in Part 1.

Grammar and syntax

Written American English tends to be more declarative than its British counterpart, and adverbs and some modifying phrases are frequently positioned differently. British English also tends to use more modifying phrases, while American English prefers to go with simpler sentence structure.

In British English, doctors and lawyers are to be found *in* Harley Street or Wall Street, not *on* it. And they rest from their labours *at* weekends, not *on* them. During the week their children are *at* school, not *in* it.

Words may also be inserted or omitted in some standard phrases. British English goes *to hospital,* American English *to the hospital.* British English chooses *one or other thing;* American English chooses *one thing or the other.*

Punctuation

commas in lists The use of a comma before the final *and* in a list is called the serial or Oxford comma: *eggs, bacon, potatoes, and cheese.* Most American writers and publishers use the serial comma; most British writers and publishers use the serial comma only when necessary to avoid ambiguity: *eggs, bacon, potatoes and cheese* but *The musicals were by Rodgers and Hammerstein, Sondheim, and Lerner and Loewe.*

full stops (periods) The American convention is to use full stops (periods) at the end of almost all abbreviations and contractions; specifically, full stops with abbreviations in lower case, *a.m., p.m.,* and no full stops with abbreviations in capitals or small capitals, US, UN, CEO. The British convention is to use full stops after abbreviations – eg, *abbr., adj., co.* – but not after contractions – eg, *Dr, Mr, Mrs, St.*

hyphens American English is far readier than British English to accept compound words. In particular, many nouns made of two separate nouns are spelt as one word in American English, while in British English they either remain separate or are joined by a hyphen: eg, *applesauce, newborn, commonsense* (hyphenated or two words in British English).

British English also tends, more than American English, to use hyphens as pronunciation aids, to separate repeated vowels in words such as *pre-empt* and *re-examine,* and to join some prefixes to nouns – eg, *pseudo-science.* Americans tend to get rid of hyphens more rapidly than the British, as new editions of dictionaries reflect.

In British English, hyphens are more frequently used in compound adjectives or adjectival phrases than in American English. *See also* **hyphens** in Part 1.

quotation marks In American publications and those of some Commonwealth countries, and also international publications like *The Economist*, the convention is to use double quotation marks, reserving single quotation marks for quotes within quotes. In many British publications (excluding *The Economist*), the convention is the reverse: single quotation marks are used first, then double.

With other punctuation the relative position of quotation marks and other punctuation also differs. The British convention is to place such punctuation according to sense. The American convention is simpler but less logical: all commas and full stops precede the final quotation mark (or, if there is a quote within a quote, the first final quotation mark). Other punctuation – colons, semi-colons, question and exclamation marks – is placed according to sense. The following examples illustrate these differences.

British

The words on the magazine's cover, *'The link between coffee and cholesterol'*, caught his eye.

'You're eating too much,' she told him. *'You'll soon look like your father.'*

'Have you seen this article, "The link between coffee and cholesterol"?' he asked.

'It was as if', he explained, *'I had swallowed a toad, and it kept croaking "ribbut, ribbut", from deep in my belly.'*

She particularly enjoyed the article *'Looking for the "New Man"'*.

American

The words on the magazine's cover, *"The link between coffee and cholesterol,"* caught his eye.

"You're eating too much," she told him. *"You'll soon look like your father."*

"Have you seen this article, 'The link between coffee and cholesterol'?" he asked.

"It was as if," he explained, *"I had swallowed a toad, and it kept croaking 'Ribbut, ribbut,' from deep in my stomach."*

She particularly enjoyed the article *"Looking for the 'New Man.'"*

Spelling

Some words are spelt differently in American English and British English. Often the American spelling is a survival of 18th-century British usage. The spellings are sufficiently similar to identify the word, but the unfamiliar form may still disturb the reader. If you are writing for an international audience, the American form is now much more likely to be recognised.

American English is more obviously phonetic than British English. The word *cosy* becomes *cozy*, *aesthetic* becomes *esthetic*, *sizeable* becomes *sizable*, *arbour* becomes *arbor*, *theatre* becomes *theater*.

Main spelling differences

-ae/-oe Although it is now common in British English to write *medieval* rather than *mediaeval*, other words – often scientific terms such as *aeon, diarrhoea, anaesthetic, gynaecology, homoeopathy* – retain their classical composite vowel. In American English, the composite vowel is replaced by a single *e*; thus, *eon, diarrhea, anesthetic, gynecology, homeopathy*. There are exceptions to this in scientific publications. *Fetus* is the preferred spelling on both sides of the Atlantic (not *foetus*), and *oestrogen* generally becomes *estrogen*, if only to ensure that the hormone appears in the same place in alphabetical lists in both countries.

-ce/-se In British English, the verb that relates to a noun ending in *-ce* is sometimes given the ending *-se*; thus, *advice* (noun), *advise* (verb), *device/devise, licence/license, practice/practise*. In the first two instances, the spelling change is accompanied by a slight change in the sound of the word; but in the other two instances, noun and verb are pronounced the same way, and American English spelling reflects this, by using the same spelling for both noun and verb: thus, *license/license* and *practise/practise*. It also extends the use of *-se* to other nouns that in British English are spelt *-ce*: thus, *defense, offense, pretense*.

-e/-ue The final silent *e* or *ue* of several words is omitted in American English but retained in British English: thus, *analog/analogue, ax/axe, catalog/catalogue*.

163

-eable/-able The silent *e*, created when forming some adjectives with this suffix, is more often omitted in American English; thus, *likeable* is spelt *likable*, *unshakeable* is spelt *unshakable*. But the *e* is sometimes retained in American English where it affects the sound of the preceding consonant; thus, *traceable* and *manageable*.

-ize/-ise The American convention is to spell with *z* many words that some British people and publishers (including *The Economist*) spell with *s*. The *z* spelling is, of course, also a correct British form. Remember, though, that some words must end in *-ise*, whichever spelling convention is being followed. These include:

advertise	despise	incise
advise	devise	merchandise
apprise	disguise	premise
arise	emprise	prise
chastise	enfranchise	revise
circumcise	excise	supervise
comprise	exercise	surmise
compromise	franchise	surprise
demise	improvise	televise

Words with the ending *-lyse* in British English, such as *analyse* and *paralyse*, are spelt *-lyze* in American English.

-ll/-l In British English, when words ending in the consonant *l* are given a suffix beginning with a vowel (eg, the suffixes *-able*, *-ed*, *-ing*, *-ous*, *-y*), the *l* is doubled; thus, *annul/annulled*, *model/modelling*, *quarrel/quarrelling*, *rebel/rebellious*, *wool/woolly*. This is inconsistent with the general rule in British English that the final consonant is doubled before the suffix only when the preceding vowel carries the main stress: thus, the word *regret* becomes *regretted*, or *regrettable*; but the word *billet* becomes *billeted*. American English mostly does not have this inconsistency. So if the stress does not fall on the preceding vowel, the *l* is not doubled: thus, *model/modeling*, *travel/traveler*; but *annul/annulled*.

Several words that end in a single *l* in British English – eg, *appal*, *fulfil* – take a double *ll* in American English. In British

English the *l* stays single when the word takes a suffix beginning
with a consonant (eg, the suffixes *-ful*, *-fully*, *-ment*): thus, *fulfil/
fulfilment*. Words ending in *-ll* usually lose one *l* when taking
one of these suffixes: thus, *skill/skilful*, *will/wilfully*. In American
English, words ending in *-ll* usually remain intact, whatever the
suffix: thus, *skill/skillful*, *will/willfully*.

-m/-mme American English tends to use the shorter form of
ending, thus *gram* and *program*, and British English tends to use
the longer: *gramme* and *programme* (but *program* when referring
to a computer program).

-our/-or Most British English words ending in *-our* – *ardour*,
behaviour, *candour*, *demeanour*, *favour*, *valour* and the like – lose
the *u* in American English: thus, *ardor*, *candor*, etc. The major
exception, though even this is broken, is *glamour*, which retains
its u (but loses it in both types of English for the adjective
glamorous). Note, however, that *squalor* is spelt the same on both
sides of the Atlantic.

-re/-er Most British English words ending in *-re* – such as *centre*,
fibre, *metre*, *theatre* – end in *-er* in American English: thus,
center, *fiber*, etc. Exceptions include: *acre*, *cadre*, *lucre*, *massacre*,
mediocre, *ogre*.

-t/-ed Although this seems to be a mere difference in spelling
the past tense of some verbs, it is really a different form; *see*
'Verbs: past tenses' below.

Other common spelling differences

British	American
aluminium	aluminum
apophthegm	apothegm
behove	behoove
chequered	checkered (pattern)
cosy	cozy
draught	draft
dyke	dike
furore	furor
grey	gray

kerb/kerbside	curb/curbside
liquorice	licorice
manoeuvre/manoeuvrable	maneuver/maneuverable
mould/moulder/moult	mold/molder/molt
moustache	mustache
plough	plow
podgy	pudgy
rumbustious	rambunctious
specialist shop	specialty store
speciality (but specialty for medicine, steel and chemicals)	specialty
sulphur(ous) (but sulfur(ous) in scientific publications)	sulfur(ous)
titbit	tidbit
towards	toward
tyre	tire
vice (tool)	vise

Usage

dates Americans are at odds with the rest of the world in the way they express dates in numerical form. In Britain and elsewhere, the order is always: day, month, year – eg, 7/9/2008 for September 7th 2008. In the United States, it is: month, day, year – eg, 9/7/2008. This can lead to misunderstanding – not least with the common term "9/11" to refer to the destruction of the World Trade Center on September 11th 2001, which the rest of the world will automatically translate as November 9th.

exclusivity What is familiar in one culture may be entirely alien in another. British English exploits terms and phrases borrowed from the game of cricket; American English uses baseball terms. Those writing for readers in both markets use either set of terms at their peril. Do not make references or assumptions that are geographically exclusive, for example by specifying months or seasons when referring to seasonal patterns, by using north or south to imply a type of climate, or by making geographical references that give a state's name followed by USA, as in *Wyoming, USA*. You can help to avoid confusion: *Cambridge, England; Cambridge, MA*.

race and sex The difficulties that arise in Europe as a result of references to race and sex (*see* ethnic groups, political correctness) are even greater in America. When referring to Americans whose ancestors came from Africa, most people use the adjective *African-American* rather than *black*. Other groups are referred to by their specific ethnicity; for instance, Hispanics, who are also *Latinos/Latinas*.

American Indians are usually called *native Americans*, not least to distinguish them from the ever-growing numbers of Indian-Americans. It is unacceptable to refer to them as *red*. It can also cause offence to describe the original inhabitants of the lands stretching from Greenland to Alaska as *Eskimos*; this was a corruption of a Cree word meaning *raw-flesh eater*. The people themselves are distributed among at least three major tribal groupings. Alaskan natives are usually called *native Americans* in Alaska. *Inuit* should be used only to refer to people of that tribe.

units of measurement In British publications measurements are now largely expressed in SI units (the modern form of metric units), although imperial measures are still used in certain contexts. In American publications measurements may be expressed in SI units, but imperial units are still more common.

Although the British imperial and American standard measures are usually identical, there are some important exceptions, eg, the number of fluid ounces in a pint: 16 in the American system and 20 in the British. This difference has a knock-on effect in the volumes of gallons, which are smaller in America than in Britain. Americans also use the measure *quart* (one-quarter of a gallon), which is now considered archaic in Britain.

Some measures are peculiar to one or other national system, particularly units of mass relating to agriculture. *See also* **measures** in Part 3.

verbs: past tenses -*t*/-*ed* Both forms of ending are acceptable in
British English, but the -*t* form is dominant – *burnt, learnt, spelt*
– whereas American English uses -*ed*: *burned, learned, spelled*.
Contrarily, British English uses –*ed* for the past tense and past
participle of certain verbs – *quitted, sweated* – while American
English uses the infinitive spelling – *quit, sweat*. Some verbs have
a different form of past tense and past participle, eg, the past
tense of *dive* is *dived* in British English but *dove* in American
English, and the past tense of *fit* is always *fit* in American
English, not *fitted*, as in British English. Although *loaned* is still
sometimes used as the past tense of *lend* in American English, it
is not standard.

Vocabulary

Sometimes the same word has gradually taken on different
meanings on the two sides of the Atlantic, creating an
opportunity for misunderstanding. The word *homely*, for
example, means *simple* or *informal* in British English, but *plain* or
unattractive in American English.

This also applies to figures of speech. *It went like a bomb*
in British English means it was a great success; *it bombed* in
American English means it was a disaster. *To table* something
in British English means to bring it forward for action; but in
American English it means the opposite, ie, *to shelve*.

One writer's slang is another's lively use of words; formal
language to one is pomposity to another. This is the trickiest area
to negotiate when writing for both British and American readers.
At its best, distinctively American English is more direct and
vivid than its British English equivalent. Many American words
and expressions have passed into British English because they
are shorter or more to the point: eg, *lay off* is preferable to *make
redundant*, and *fire* is preferable to *dismiss*. But American English
also has a contrary tendency to lengthen words, creating a (to
British readers) pompous tone: for instance, *transportation* (in
British English, *transport*).

British English is slower than American English to accept
new words and suspicious of short cuts, and sometimes it resists
the use of nouns as verbs (*see* **grammar and syntax** in Part 1).

The following lists draw attention to commonly used words and idioms that are spelt differently or have different meanings in American English and British English. When you do not want to produce a single version, follow one or other convention and, if this means using a word that will mystify or mislead one group of readers, provide a translation. The lists do not cover slang or colloquialisms.

accounting, banking and finance

British	American
acquisition accounting	purchase accounting
articles of association	bylaws
banknote	bill
bonus or scrip issue	stock dividend or stock split
building society	savings and loan association
Chartered Accountant (CA)	Certified Public Accountant (CPA)
cheque (bank)	check
clerk (bank)	teller
closing rate method	current rate method
current account	checking account
deferred tax	deferred income tax
depreciation	amortisation
exceptional items	unusual items
finance leases	capital leases
HM Revenue and Customs (HMRC)/Inland Revenue	Internal Revenue
property	real estate
nominal value	par value
non-pension post-employment benefits	OPEBS (other post-employment benefits)
old-age pension, state pension	Social Security
ordinary shares	common stock
pay rise	raise
preference shares	preferred stock
price rise	price hike
profit for the financial year	net income
provisions	allowances
share premium	additional paid-in capital

shareholders' funds	stockholders' equity
stock	inventory
Treasury share	Treasury stock
turnover	revenues
undistributable reserves	restricted surplus or deficiency
unit trust	mutual fund
value-added tax (VAT)	sales tax

baby items

British	*American*
baby's dummy	pacifier
cot	crib
nappy	diaper
pram, push-chair	baby carriage, stroller

clothes

British	*American*
braces	suspenders
clothes cupboard/wardrobe	closet
dressing gown	bathrobe/housecoat/robe
hairgrips	bobby pins
handbag, wallet	purse, pocketbook
ladder (in stocking)	run
pants	underpants
press studs	snaps
purse	wallet
sports jacket	sport jacket
tartan	plaid
tights	pantyhose, (opaque) tights
trousers	pants, slacks, trousers
vest	undershirt
waistcoat	vest
zip (noun)	zipper

food, cooking and eating

British	*American*
aubergine	eggplant
bill (restaurant)	check

biscuit (sweet)	cookie
biscuit (savoury)	cracker
black treacle	molasses
chips	French fries
cling film	plastic wrap
cooker	stove
coriander	cilantro
cornflour	cornstarch
courgette	zucchini
crayfish	crawfish
crisps	potato chips
crystallised	candied
double cream	heavy cream
essence (eg, vanilla)	extract or flavoring
flour, plain	flour, all-purpose
flour, self-raising	flour, self-rising
flour, wholemeal	flour, whole-wheat
golden syrup	corn syrup
greengrocer's	fruit and vegetable store
grill (verb and noun)	broil (verb), broiler (noun)
icing sugar	powdered or confectioners' sugar
main course	entrée
maize/sweetcorn	corn
mince	hamburger meat
minced meat	ground meat
pastry case	pie crust
pepper (red, green, etc)	sweet pepper, bell pepper, capsicum
pips	seeds (in fruit)
rocket (salad)	arugula
shortcrust pastry	short pastry/basic pie dough
single cream	light cream
soya	soy
spring onion	scallion, green onion
starter	appetizer
stoned (cherries, etc)	pitted
sultana	golden raisin
sweet shop	candy store
water biscuit	cracker

homes and other buildings

British	American
camp bed	cot
cinema	movie theater
council estate	public housing or project
flat	apartment
ground floor	first floor
home from home	home away from home
homely	homey
housing estate	housing development
lavatory, toilet	bathroom, restroom, washroom
lift	elevator
power point	electrical outlet, socket
property (land)	real estate
storey	story, floor
terraced house	row house

people, professions and politics

British	American
adopt a candidate	nominate a candidate
barrister	trial lawyer
doctor	physician
estate agent	realtor/real estate agent
ex-serviceman	veteran
headmistress/headmaster	principal
jeweller/jewellery	jeweler/jewelry
lawyer	attorney
manifesto (political)	platform
old-age pensioner, OAP	senior citizen, senior
sceptic	skeptic
senior (politician)	ranking
solicitor	attorney, lawyer
stand for office	run for office

travel, transport and pedestrians

British	American
accelerator	gas pedal
bonnet, car	hood

boot, car	trunk
bumper	fender
car park	parking lot
caravan	trailer, motorhome, RV
coach	bus
crossroads/junction	intersection
cul-de-sac	dead end
demister	defogger
driving licence	driver's license
dual carriageway	divided highway
estate car	station wagon
exhaust, car	muffler
flyover	overpass
gearbox	transmission
give way	yield
high street	main street
hire (a car)	rent or hire
indicator	turn signal
jump leads	jumper cables
lorry	truck
motor-racing	auto-racing
motorway	highway, freeway, expressway, thruway
number plate	license plate
passenger	rider
pavement	sidewalk
pedestrian crossing	crosswalk
petrol	gasoline, gas
petrol station	gas/service station
puncture	flat tire
railway station	train station
rambler	hiker
return ticket	round-trip ticket
riding (horses)	horseback riding
ring road	beltway
road surface	pavement
rowing boat	rowboat
sailing boat	sailboat

single ticket	one-way ticket
slip road	ramp
subway	pedestrian underpass
transport	transportation
turning (road)	turnoff
underground (or tube train)	subway
walk	hike (only if more energetic than a walk)
windscreen	windshield

other words and phrases

British	*American*
aerial (TV)	antenna
ageing	aging
anti-clockwise	counterclockwise
at weekends	on weekends
autumn	fall
bank holiday	public holiday
British Summer Time (BST)	Daylight Saving Time (DST)
chemist	drugstore, pharmacy
clever	smart (though since everything digital is smart, this usage is becoming almost universal in British English)
diary (appointments)	calendar
diary (record)	journal
dustbin	garbage can
earthed (wire)	ground
film	movie
flannel	washcloth
fortnight	two weeks
from ... to ...	through (with the understanding that the period terminates at the end of the day, month or year)
got (past participle)	gotten
holiday	vacation
lease of life	lease on life
mean (parsimonious)	stingy, tight (mean is nasty, cruel)

mobile phone	cell phone
oblige	obligate
ordinary	regular, normal
outside	outside of
over (as in too much)	overly
paddling pool	wading pool
plait	braid
post, post box	mail, mailbox
post code	zip code
postponement	rain-check
public school	private school
queue (noun and verb)	line (noun), line up
quite	somewhat (quite means very)
reverse charges	call collect
phone	call, phone
spanner	wrench
state school	public school
stupid	dumb
torch	flashlight
upmarket	upscale
work out (problem)	figure out
Zimmer frame	walker
zed (the letter z)	zee

Below is a list of words that are acceptable in both American and British English, for use when you want to produce a single version of written material for both categories of reader.

ambience *not* ambiance
among *not* amongst
annex *not* annexe
artifact *not* artefact
backward *not* backwards
baptistry *not* baptistery
Bible, *not* bible (for *Scriptures*)
burned *not* burnt
bus *not* coach
canvases *not* canvasses
car rental *not* car hire

cater to *not* cater for (for needs)
custom-made *not* bespoke
development *not* estate (for housing)
diesel fuel *not* DERV
disc *not* disk (except in computing)
dispatch *not* despatch
encyclopedia *not* encyclopaedia
except for *not* save
farther *not* further (for distance)
first name *not* Christian name
flip *not* toss (for coins, etc)
focusing, focused, etc
forward *not* forwards
fuel *not* petrol (UK) *or* gasoline (US)
(eye)glasses *not* spectacles
gypsy *not* gipsy
hairdryer *not* hairdrier
horse-racing *not just* racing
insurance coverage *not* insurance cover
intermission *not* interval
jail *not* gaol
learned *not* learnt
line *not* queue
location *not* situation
maid *not* chambermaid
mathematics *not* maths (UK) *or* math (US)
motorcycle *not* motorbike
neat *not* spruce *or* tidy
news-stand *not* kiosk
nightgown *not* nightdress
orangeade/lemonade *not* orange/lemon squash
package *not* parcel
parking spaces/garage *not* car park (UK) *or* parking lot (US)
phoney *not* phony
refrigerator *not* fridge
railway *not* railroad
raincoat *not* mac, mackintosh
rent *not* hire (except for people)

reservation, reserve (seats, etc) *not* booking, book
retired person *not* old-age pensioner (UK) *or* retiree (US)
slowdown *not* go-slow (in production)
soccer *not* football (except for American football)
spelled *not* spelt
spoiled *not* spoilt
street musician *not* busker
swap *not* swop
swimming *not* bathing
team *not* side (in sport)
tearoom *not* teashop
thread *not* cotton
toilet *not* lavatory
toll-free *not* free of charge (for telephone numbers)
tuna *not* tunny
underwear *not* pants or knickers (or use lingerie for women's
underwear)
unmistakable *not* unmistakeable
unspoiled *not* unspoilt
while *not* whilst
yogurt *not* yoghourt *or* yoghurt
zero *not* nought

part 3

Useful reference

Abbreviations

Here is a list of some common business abbreviations.

See also **abbreviations** in Part 1, **technology**, pages 259–62.

ABC	activity-based costing
ACH	automated clearing house
ADR	American depositary receipt
AG	Aktiengesellschaft (Austrian, German or Swiss public limited company)
AGM	annual general meeting
AIBD	Association of International Bond Dealers
AIM	Alternative Investment Market (UK)
AMEX	American Stock Exchange
APR	annualised percentage rate (of interest)
APT	arbitrage pricing theory
ARPU	average revenue per user/unit
ARR	accounting rate of return
ASB	Accounting Standards Board (UK)
B2B	business-to-business
B2C	business-to-consumer
BACS	bankers' automated clearing services
BPO	business process outsourcing
BPR	business process re-engineering
CAGR	compound average growth rate
CAPM	capital asset pricing model
CCA	current cost accounting
CD	certificate of deposit

CDO	collateralised debt obligation
CDS	credit-default swap
CEO	chief executive officer
CFO	chief financial officer
CHAPS	Clearing House Automated Payments System
CIF	cost, insurance, freight
CIO	chief information officer
COB	Commission des Opérations de Bourse (Stock Exchange Commission, France)
Consob	Commissione Nazionale per le Società e la Borsa (Italian Securities and Exchange Commission)
COO	chief operating officer
COLA	cost of living adjustment
COSA	cost of sales adjustment
CPA	certified public accountant (US); critical path analysis
CPP	current purchasing power (accounting)
CRC	current replacement cost (or replacement cost)
CRM	customer relationship management
CSR	corporate social responsibility
CTO	chief technology officer; configure to order
CVP	cost-volume-profit analysis
DCF	discounted cash flow
EBIT	earnings before interest and tax
EBITDA	earnings before interest, tax, depreciation and amortisation
ECN	electronic communication network
EDI	electronic data interchange
EDLP	every day low price
EDP	electronic data processing
EFT	electronic funds transfer
EFTPOS	electronic funds transfer at point of sale
EOQ	economic order quantity
EPS	earnings per share
ERM	enterprise resource management
ESOP	employee stock (or share) ownership plan
ETF	exchange-traded fund

Euribor	Euro Interbank Offered Rate
EV	enterprise value
EVA	economic value added
FAS	financial accounting standards (US)
FASB	Financial Accounting Standards Board (US)
FCA	Financial Conduct Authority (UK)
FDI	foreign direct investment
FDIC	Federal Deposit Insurance Corporation (US)
FIFO	first in, first out (used for valuing stock/inventory)
FMCG	fast-moving consumer goods
FMS	flexible management system
fob	free on board
FRN	floating-rate note
FTE	full-time equivalent
FY	fiscal year
GAAP	generally accepted accounting principles (US)
GAAS	generally accepted audited standards
GDP	gross domestic product
GmbH	Gesellschaft mit beschränkter Haftung (Austrian, German or Swiss private limited company)
GNI	gross national income
GNP	gross national product
GPS	global positioning system
IAASB	International Auditing and Assurance Standards Board
IAS	international accounting standards
IASB	International Accounting Standards Board
IBF	international banking facility
ICGN	International Corporate Governance Network
ICMA	International Capital Market Association
IFA	independent financial adviser
IFRS	International Financial Reporting Standards
ILO	International Labour Organisation
IOSCO	International Organisation of Securities Commissions
IPO	initial public offering
IRR	internal rate of return
IRS	Internal Revenue Service (US)

ISA	individual savings account; International Standards on Auditing
ISO	International Organisation for Standardisation
JIT	just-in-time
KPI	key performance indicator
LBO	leveraged buy-out
Libor	London Interbank Offered Rate
LIFO	last in, first out (used for valuing stock/inventory value, popular in US)
LLP	limited liability partnership
LNG	liquefied natural gas
LPG	liquefied petroleum gas
LSE	London Stock Exchange
M&A	mergers and acquisitions
MBI	management buy-in
MBO	management buy-out
MLR	minimum lending rate (base rate)
MOU	memorandum of understanding
MSRP	manufacturer's suggested retail price
NASDAQ	National Association of Securities Dealers Automatic Quotation System (US)
NAV	net asset value
NBV	net book value
NGO	non-governmental organisation
NPV	net present value; no par value
NRV	net realisable value
NYMEX	New York Mercantile Exchange
NYSE	New York Stock Exchange
OBU	offshore banking unit
OCR	optical character recognition
OEIC	open-ended investment company
OEM	original equipment manufacturer
OFR	operating and financial review
OTC	over the counter
P/B	price to book value
PCAOB	Public Company Accounting Oversight Board

P/E	price/earnings ratio
PLC	public limited company (UK)
PPP	purchasing-power parity; public–private partnership
PSBR	public-sector borrowing requirement
QE	quantitative easing
R&D	research and development
REIT	real-estate investment trust
RFID	radio-frequency identification
RNOA	return on net operating assets
ROA	return on assets
ROCE	return on capital employed
ROE	return on equity
ROI	return on investment
RONA	return on net assets
ROTA	return on total assets
RPI	retail price index
RPIX	retail price index excluding mortgage interest payments
RTM	route to market
S&L	Savings and Loan Association (US)
SA	société anonyme (French, Belgian, Luxembourg or Swiss public limited company)
Sarl	société à responsabilité limitée (French, etc private limited company)
SBU	strategic business unit
SCM	supply-chain management
SDR	special drawing right (at the IMF)
SE	Societas Europaea
SEAQ	Stock Exchange Automated Quotations (UK)
SEC	Securities and Exchange Commission (US)
SET	secure electronic transaction
SFO	Serious Fraud Office (UK)
SITC	standard international trade classification
SMART	specific, measurable, achievable, realistic, time bound
SME	small- and medium-sized enterprises
SOE	state-owned enterprise
SOHO	small office/home office

SOX	Sarbanes-Oxley Act (US)
SPA	società per azioni (Italian public company)
SPV	special purpose vehicle
SRO	self-regulatory organisation
SPV/SPE	special-purpose vehicle/entity
SSAP	Statement of Standard Accounting Practice (UK)
STRGL	statement of total recognised gains and losses
SWF	sovereign-wealth fund
SWIFT	Society for Worldwide Interbank Financial Telecommunication
SWOT	strengths, weaknesses, opportunities, threats
T-bill	Treasury bill
TSR	total shareholder return
UCITS	Undertakings for Collective Investments in Transferable Securities
USP	unique selling proposition/point
VAT	value-added tax
VCT	venture capital trust
VIX	stockmarket volatility index
WACC	weighted average cost of capital
WDV	written-down value
WFH	work from home
WIP	work in progress
XBRL	extensible business reporting language
YTD	year to date
YTM	yield to maturity
ZBB	zero-base budgeting

For international bodies and their abbreviations, *see* **organisations**, pages 232–47.

Beaufort Scale

For devotees of the shipping forecast, here is the World Meteorological Organisation's classification of wind forces and effects.

Conditions (abbreviated)				Equivalent speed at 10m height		
Force	Description	On land	At sea	knots	miles per hour	metres per second
0	Calm	Smoke rises vertically	Sea like a mirror	less than 1	less than 1	0.0–0.2
1	Light air	Smoke drifts	Ripples	1–3	1–3	0.3–1.5
2	Light breeze	Leaves rustle	Small wavelets	4–6	4–7	1.6–3.3
3	Gentle breeze	Wind extends light flag	Large wavelets, crests break	7–10	8–12	3.4–5.4
4	Moderate breeze	Raises paper and dust	Small waves, fairly frequent white horses	11–16	13–18	5.5–7.9
5	Fresh breeze	Small trees in leaf sway	Moderate waves, many white horses	17–21	19–24	8.0–10.7
6	Strong breeze	Large branches in motion	Large waves form, some spray	22–27	25–31	10.8–13.8
7	Near gale	Whole trees in motion	Sea heaps up, white foam streaks	28–33	32–38	13.9–17.1
8	Gale	Breaks twigs off trees	Moderately high waves, well-marked foam streaks	34–40	39–46	17.2–20.7

Conditions (abbreviated)				Equivalent speed at 10m height		
Force	Description	On land	At sea	knots	miles per hour	metres per second
9	Strong gale	Slight structural damage	High waves, crests start to tumble over	41–47	47–54	20.8–24.4
10	Storm	Trees uprooted, considerable structural damage	Very high waves, white sea tumbles	48–55	55–63	24.5–28.4
11	Violent storm	Very rarely experienced, widespread damage	Exceptionally high waves, edges of wave crests blown to froth	56–63	64–72	28.5–32.6
12–17	Hurricane	Devastation with driving spray	Sea completely white	64–over	72–over	32.7–over

Business ratios

These are ratios commonly used in corporate financial analysis.

Working capital

Working capital ratio = current assets/current liabilities, where current assets = inventory + receivables + cash at bank and in hand + quoted investments, etc, and current liabilities = payables + short-term bank borrowing + taxes payable + dividends, etc. The ratio varies according to type of trade and conditions; a ratio from 1 to 3 is usual with a ratio above 2 taken to be safe.

Liquidity ratio = liquid ("quick") assets/current liabilities, where liquid assets = receivables + cash at bank and in hand + quoted investments (that is, assets that can be realised within a month or so, which may not apply to all investments); current liabilities are those that may need to be repaid within the same short period, which may not necessarily include a bank overdraft where it is likely to be renewed. The liquidity ratio is sometimes referred to as the "acid test"; a ratio under 1 suggests a possibly difficult situation, and too high a ratio may mean that assets are not being usefully employed.

Turnover of working capital = sales/average working capital. The ratio varies according to type of trade; generally a low ratio can mean poor use of resources, and too high a ratio can mean overtrading. Average working capital or average inventory is found by taking the opening and closing working capital or inventory and dividing by 2.

Turnover of inventory = sales/average inventory, or (where cost of sales is known) cost of sales/average inventory. The cost of sales turnover figure is to be preferred, as both figures are then on the same valuation basis. This ratio can be expressed as number of times per year, or time taken for inventory to be turned over once = (52/number of times) weeks. A low inventory turnover can be a sign of inventory items that are difficult to move, and usually indicates adverse conditions.

Turnover of receivables = sales/average receivables. This indicates efficiency in collecting accounts. An average credit period of about one month is usual, but this varies according to credit stringency conditions in the economy.

Turnover of payables = purchases/average payables. Average payment period is best maintained in line with turnover of receivables.

Sales

Export ratio = exports as a percentage of sales.

Sales per employee = sales/average number of employees.

Assets

Ratios of assets can vary according to the measure of assets used:

Total assets = current assets + non-current assets + other assets, where non-current assets = property + plant and equipment + motor vehicles, etc, and other assets = long-term investment + goodwill, etc.

Net assets ("net worth") = total assets minus total liabilities = share capital + reserves = equity.

Turnover of net assets = sales/average net assets. As for turnover of working capital, a low ratio can mean poor use of resources.

Assets per employee = assets/average number of employees. This indicates the amount of investment backing for employees.

Profits

Profit margin = (profit/sales) × 100 = profits as a percentage of sales; usually profits before tax.

Profitability = (profit/total assets) × 100 = profits as a percentage of total assets = return on total assets (ROTA).

Return on capital = (profit/net assets) × 100 = profits as a percentage of net assets ("net worth", "equity" or "capital employed") = return on net assets (RONA), return on equity (ROE) or return on capital employed (ROCE).

Profit per employee = profit/average number of employees.

Earnings per share (EPS) = after-tax profit minus minorities/average number of shares in issue.

Central bankers since 1900

Governors of the Bank of England

Date	Governor
1899–1901	Samuel Gladstone
1901–03	Augustus Prevost
1903–05	Samuel Morley
1905–07	Alexander Wallace
1907–09	William Campbell
1909–11	Reginald Johnston
1911–13	Alfred Cole
1913–18	Walter Cunliffe
1918–20	Brien Cokayne
1920–44	Montagu Norman
1944–49	Thomas Catto
1949–61	Cameron Cobbold
1961–66	Rowland Baring (3rd Earl of Cromer)
1966–73	Leslie O'Brien
1973–83	Gordon Richardson
1983–93	Robert Leigh-Pemberton
1993–2003	Edward George
2003–2013	Mervyn King
2013–	Mark Carney

Chairs of the United States Federal Reserve (since the creation of the Federal Reserve System in 1913)

Date	Chair
1914–16	Charles Hamlin
1916–22	William P.G. Harding
1923–27	Daniel R. Crissinger
1927–30	Roy A. Young
1930–33	Eugene Meyer
1933–34	Eugene Black
1934–48	Marriner Eccles
1948–51	Thomas B. McCabe
1951–70	William McChesney
1970–78	Arthur Burns
1978–79	William Miller
1979–87	Paul Volcker
1987–2006	Alan Greenspan
2006–14	Ben Bernanke
2014–	Janet Yellen

Managing Directors of the International Monetary Fund (since its creation in 1945)

Date	Managing Director
1946–51	Camille Gutt
1951–56	Ivar Rooth
1956–63	Per Jacobsson
1963–73	Pierre-Paul Schweitzer
1973–87	Johan Witteveen
1987–2000	Michel Camdessus
2000–2004	Horst Köhler
2004–07	Rodrigo Rato
2007–11	Dominique Strauss-Kahn
2011–	Christine Lagarde

Presidents of the European Central Bank since its creation in 1998

Date	President
1998–2003	Wim Duisenberg
2003–11	Jean-Claude Trichet
2011–	Mario Draghi

Presidents of the World Bank since its creation in 1945

Date	President
1945–46	Eugene Meyer
1947–49	John J. McCloy
1949–63	Eugene R. Black, Sr.
1963–68	George Woods
1968–81	Robert McNamara
1981–86	Alden W. Clausen
1986–91	Barber Conable
1991–95	Lewis T. Preston
1995–2005	James D. Wolfensohn
2005–07	Paul Wolfowitz
2007–12	Zoellick, Robert
2012–	Jim Yong Kim

Currencies

See also **currencies** in Part 1 for *The Economist* newspaper usage.

Country	Currency	Symbol
Afghanistan	afghani	Af
Albania	lek	Lk
Algeria	Algerian dinar	AD
Angola	kwanza	Kz
Argentina	Argentine peso	Ps
Armenia	dram	Dram
Aruba	Aruban florin	Afl
Australia	Australian dollar	A$

Country	Currency	Symbol
Austria	euro	€
Azerbaijan	manat	Manat
Bahamas	Bahamian dollar	B$
Bahrain	Bahraini dinar	BD
Bangladesh	taka	Tk
Barbados	Barbados dollar	Bd$
Belarus	ruble	BRb
Belgium	euro	€
Belize	Belize dollar	Bz$
Benin	CFA franc	CFAfr[a]
Bermuda	Bermuda dollar	Bda$
Bhutan	ngultrum	Nu
Bolivia	boliviano	Bs
Bosnia & Herzegovina	convertible marka	KM
Botswana	pula	P
Brazil	Brazilian real	R
Brunei	Brunei dollar/ringgit	Br$
Bulgaria	lev	Lv
Burkina Faso	CFA franc	CFAfr[a]
Burundi	Burundi franc	Bufr
Cambodia	riel	CR
Cameroon	CFA franc	CFAfr[a]
Canada	Canadian dollar	C$
Cape Verde	Cape Verdean escudo	CVEsc
Central African Republic	CFA franc	CFAfr[a]
Chad	CFA franc	CFAfr[a]
Chile	Chilean peso	Ps
China	renminbi or yuan	Rmb
Colombia	Colombian peso	Ps
Comoros	Comorian franc	Cfr

Country	Currency	Symbol
Congo (Brazzaville)	CFA franc	CFAfr[a]
Congo (Dem. Rep. of)	Congolese franc	FC
Costa Rica	Costa Rican colón	C
Croatia	kuna	HRK
Cuba	Cuban peso	CUPs
Cyprus	euro	€
Czech Republic	koruna	Kc
Denmark	Danish krone	DKr
Djibouti	Djibouti franc	Dfr
Dominican Republic	Dominican Republic peso	Ps
East Timor	US dollar	US$
Ecuador	US dollar	US$
Egypt	Egyptian pound	E£
El Salvador	US dollar	US$
Equatorial Guinea	CFA franc	CFAfr[a]
Eritrea	nakfa	Nfa
Estonia	euro	€
Ethiopia	birr	Birr
Fiji	Fiji dollar	F$
Finland	euro	€
France	euro	€
Gabon	CFA franc	CFAfr[a]
The Gambia	dalasi	D
Georgia	lari	Lari
Germany	euro	€
Ghana	cedi	GH¢
Greece	euro	€
Grenada	East Caribbean dollar	EC$
Guatemala	quetzal	Q
Guinea	Guinean franc	Gnf
Guinea-Bissau	CFA franc	CFAfr[a]

Country	Currency	Symbol
Guyana	Guyana dollar	G$
Haiti	gourde	G
Honduras	lempira	La
Hong Kong	Hong Kong dollar	HK$
Hungary	forint	Ft
Iceland	krona	IKr
India	Indian rupee	Rs
Indonesia	rupiah	Rp
Iran	Iranian rial	IR
Iraq	New Iraqi dinar	ID
Ireland	euro	€
Israel	Israeli shekel	NIS
Italy	euro	€
Ivory Coast	CFA franc	CFAfr[a]
Jamaica	Jamaican dollar	J$
Japan	yen	¥
Jordan	Jordanian dinar	JD
Kazakhstan	tenge	Tenge
Kenya	Kenyan shilling	KSh
Kyrgyzstan	som	Som
North Korea	won or N Korean won	Won
South Korea	won or S Korean won	W
Kuwait	Kuwaiti dinar	KD
Laos	kip	K
Latvia	euro	€
Lebanon	Lebanese pound	L£
Lesotho	loti (pl. maloti)	M
Liberia	Liberian dollar	L$
Libya	Libyan dinar	LD
Lithuania	euro	€
Luxembourg	euro	€

Country	Currency	Symbol
Macau	pataca	MPtc
Macedonia	denar	Den
Madagascar	Malagasy ariary	AR
Malawi	kwacha	MK
Malaysia	Malaysian dollar/ringgit	M$
Mali	CFA franc	CFAfr[a]
Malta	euro	€
Mauritania	ouguiya	UM
Mauritius	Mauritius rupee	MRs
Mexico	Mexican peso	Ps
Moldova	Moldavian leu (pl. lei)	Lei
Mongolia	togrog	Tg
Montenegro	euro	€
Morocco	dirham	Dh
Mozambique	metical	MT
Myanmar	kyat	Kt
Namibia	Namibian dollar	N$
Nepal	Nepali rupee	NRs
Netherlands	euro	€
Netherlands Antilles	Netherlands Antillean guilder	NAf
New Caledonia	French Pacific franc	CFPfr
New Zealand	New Zealand dollar	NZ$
Nicaragua	córdoba	C
Niger	CFA franc	CFAfr[a]
Nigeria	naira	N
Norway	Norwegian krone	NKr
Oman	Omani riyal	OR
Pakistan	Pakistan rupee	PRs
Palestinian Territories	Jordanian dinar, New Israeli shekel	JD, NIS
Panama	balboa	B

Country	Currency	Symbol
Papua New Guinea	kina	Kina
Paraguay	guaraní	G
Peru	nuevo sol	Ns
Philippines	Philippine peso	P
Poland	zloty (pl. zlotys)	Zl
Portugal	euro	€
Puerto Rico	US dollar	US$
Qatar	Qatari riyal	QR
Romania	leu (pl. lei)	Lei
Russia	rouble	Rb
Rwanda	Rwandan franc	Rwfr
Samoa	tala or Samoan dollar	Tala
São Tomé & Príncipe	dobra	Db
Saudi Arabia	Saudi riyal	SR
Senegal	CFA franc	CFAfr[a]
Serbia	Serbian dinar	RSD
Seychelles	Seychelles rupee	SRs
Sierra Leone	leone	Le
Singapore	Singapore dollar	S$
Slovakia	euro	€
Slovenia	euro	€
Solomon Islands	Solomon Islands dollar	SI$
Somalia	Somali shilling	SoSh
South Africa	rand	R
South Sudan	South Sudanese pound	SSP
Spain	euro	€
Sri Lanka	Sri Lankan rupee	SLRs
Sudan	Sudanese pound	SP
Suriname	Surinamese dollar	Sr$
Swaziland	lilangeni (pl. emalangeni)	E
Sweden	Swedish krona	SKr

Country	Currency	Symbol
Switzerland	Swiss franc	SFr
Syria	Syrian pound	S£
Taiwan	New Taiwan dollar	NT$
Tajikistan	somoni	S
Tanzania	Tanzanian shilling	TSh
Thailand	baht	Bt
Togo	CFA franc	CFAfr[a]
Tonga	pa'anga or Tonga dollar	T$
Trinidad & Tobago	Trinidad & Tobago dollar	TT$
Tunisia	Tunisian dinar	TD
Turkey	Turkish lira	TL
Turkmenistan	manat	Manat
Turks & Caicos Islands	US dollar	US$
Uganda	Ugandan shilling	USh
Ukraine	hryvnia	HRN
United Arab Emirates	UAE dirham	Dh
United Kingdom	pound/pound sterling	£
United States	dollar	US$
Uruguay	Uruguayan peso	Ps
Uzbekistan	som	Som
Vanuatu	vatu	Vt
Venezuela	bolívar	BsF
Vietnam	dong	D
Western Samoa	tala	Tala
Windward & Leeward Islands[b]	East Caribbean dollar	EC$
Yemen	Yemeni riyal	YR
Zambia	kwacha	ZK
Zimbabwe	Zimbabwean dollar	Z$

a CFA = Communauté financière africaine in West African area and Coopération financière en Afrique centrale in Central African area. Used in monetary areas of West and Central Africa. The CFA franc is pegged to the euro at a rate of

CFAfr655.96:€1. Countries with this currency are members of the Comité monétaire de la Zone Franc, or Franc Zone.

b Antigua and Barbuda, Dominica, Grenada, Montserrat, St Kitts-Nevis, St Lucia, St Vincent & Grenadines, the British Virgin islands.

Earthquakes

An earthquake is measured in terms of its magnitude.

Magnitude	Joules	Explosion equivalent TNT terms	Nuclear terms
0[a]	7.9×10^2	175mg	
1	6.0×10^4	13g	
2	4.0×10^6	0.89kg	
3	2.4×10^8	53kg	
4	1.3×10^{10}	3 tons	
5[b]	6.3×10^{11}	140 tons	
6[c]	2.7×10^{13}	6 kilotons	$1/3$ atomic bomb
7	1.1×10^{15}	240 kilotons	12 atomic bombs
8	3.7×10^{16}	8.25 megatons	$1/3$ hydrogen bomb
9	1.1×10^{18}	250 megatons	13 hydrogen bombs
10	3.2×10^{19}	7,000 megatons	350 hydrogen bombs

a About equal to the shock caused by an average man jumping from a table.
b Potentially damaging to structures.
c Potentially capable of general destruction; widespread damage is usually caused above magnitude 6.5.

Here are some examples.

	Magnitude
Samoa Islands, 2009	8.0
Solomon Islands, 2007	8.1
Banda Sea, Indonesia, 1938	8.5
Chile, 1906	8.5
Kamchatka, 1923	8.5

	Magnitude
Kuril Islands, 1963	8.5
Ningxia-Gansu, China, 1920	8.6
Sanriku, Japan, 1933	8.6
India/Assam/Tibet, 1950	8.7
Rat Islands, Alaska	8.7

	Magnitude		Magnitude
Northern Sumatra, 2005	8.7	Honshu, Japan, 2011	9.0
Ecuador, 1906	8.8	Andreanof Islands, Alaska,	
Chile, 2010	8.8	1957	9.1
Kamchatka, 1952	9.0	Prince William Sound, Alaska,	
Northern Sumatra, 2004		1964	9.2
(called the Indian Ocean		Chile, 1960	9.5
tsunami)	9.0	Krakatoa, 1883 (estimate)	9.9

Elements

These are the natural and artificially created chemical elements.

Name	Symbol	Atomic number	Name	Symbol	Atomic number
Actinium	Ac	89	Chlorine	Cl	17
Aluminium	Al	13	Chromium	Cr	24
Americium	Am	95	Cobalt	Co	27
Antimony (Stibium)	Sb	51	Copper (Cuprum)	Cu	29
Argon	Ar	18	Curium	Cm	96
Arsenic	As	33			
Astatine	At	85	Darmstadtium	Ds	110
			Dubnium	Db	105
Barium	Ba	56	Dysprosium	Dy	66
Berkelium	Bk	97			
Beryllium	Be	4	Einsteinium	Es	99
Bismuth	Bi	83	Erbium	Er	68
Bohrium	Bh	107	Europium	Eu	63
Boron	B	5	Fermium	Fm	100
Bromine	Br	35	Fluorine	F	9
			Francium	Fr	87
Cadmium	Cd	48			
Caesium	Cs	55	Gadolinium	Gd	64
Calcium	Ca	20	Gallium	Ga	31
Californium	Cf	98	Germanium	Ge	32
Carbon	C	6	Gold (Aurum)	Au	79
Cerium	Ce	58			

Name	Symbol	Atomic number	Name	Symbol	Atomic number
Hafnium	Hf	72	Nitrogen	N	7
Hassium	Hs	108	Nobelium	No	102
Helium	He	2			
Holmium	Ho	67	Osmium	Os	76
Hydrogen	H	1	Oxygen	O	8
Indium	In	49	Palladium	Pd	46
Iodine	I	53	Phosphorus	P	15
Iridium	Ir	77	Platinum	Pt	78
Iron (Ferrum)	Fe	26	Plutonium	Pu	94
			Polonium	Po	84
Krypton	Kr	36	Potassium (Kalium)	K	19
Lanthanum	La	57	Praseodymium	Pr	59
Lawrencium	Lr	103	Promethium	Pm	61
Lead (Plumbum)	Pb	82	Protactinium	Pa	91
Lithium	Li	3	Radium	Ra	88
Lutetium	Lu	71	Radon	Rn	86
			Rhenium	Re	75
Magnesium	Mg	12	Rhodium	Rh	45
Manganese	Mn	25	Rubidium	Rb	37
Meitnerium	Mt	109	Ruthenium	Ru	44
Mendelevium	Md	101	Rutherfordium	Rf	104
Mercury (Hydrargyrum)	Hg	80			
			Samarium	Sm	62
Molybdenum	Mo	42	Scandium	Sc	21
			Seaborgium	Sg	106
Neodymium	Nd	60	Selenium	Se	34
Neon	Ne	10	Silicon	Si	14
Neptunium	Np	93	Silver (Argentum)	Ag	47
Nickel	Ni	28			
Niobium (Columbium)	Nb	41	Sodium (Natrium)	Na	11

Name	Symbol	Atomic number	Name	Symbol	Atomic number
Strontium	Sr	38	Ununoctium	Uuo	118
Sulphur	S	16	Ununpentium	Uup	115
			Ununquadium	Uuq	114
Tantalum	Ta	73	Ununseptium	Uus	117
Technetium	Tc	43	Ununtrium	Uut	113
Tellurium	Te	52	Unununium	Uuu	111
Terbium	Tb	65	Uranium	U	92
Thallium	Tl	81			
Thorium	Th	90	Vanadium	V	23
Thulium	Tm	69			
Tin (Stannum)	Sn	50	Xenon	Xe	54
Titanium	Ti	22			
Tungsten	W	74	Ytterbium	Yb	70
(Wolfram)			Yttrium	Y	39
Ununbium	Uub	112	Zinc	Zn	30
Ununhexium	UUh	116	Zirconium	Zr	40

Footnotes, sources, references

Footnotes appear at the foot of the page (or column) on which they occur; endnotes are listed at the end of a chapter or in one batch at the end of the work. The method depends on the publisher's conventions, the type of work and the readership. The author may have little say in the matter. Footnotes may also contain additional snippets of material or comment that the author feels is not appropriate to the main text.

1 Charts, tables and figures: place source underneath.
2 Page numbers: "page" is usually abbreviated to p., plural pp., except, for example, in *The Economist*, where these are written in full.
3 Footnote numbers, which are conventionally superscript, go after the punctuation in English works, before in American. If there are not many footnotes, some publishers prefer to use asterisks, daggers, etc.

The main methods (other than *The Economist*'s) of referring to sources are: the author–date (Harvard) system; the number-only (Vancouver) system; and the author–title system.

The Economist Books should be in quotation marks, periodicals, blogs and online magazines in italics, authors, publishers, addresses (optional) and prices in roman. Commas should follow the title and the publisher (if an address is given). The other elements should each be followed by a full stop.
"A Child's Guide to the Dismal Science", by Rupert Penandwig. Haphazard House, 1234 Madison Avenue, New York, NY 10019. $28.

In charts and tables, no final stop is necessary.

Harvard system The most commonly used system in physical- and social-science publications. The author's name and year of publication appear in parentheses in the text with the full details at the end of the publication in a list of references. For example:
The variety of wildlife in our gardens (Murphy 2015) is amazing ...

In his research, Murphy (2015) finds that ...

If you wish to include the page numbers, write Murphy 2015: 165 or Murphy 2015, p. 165 or pp. 165–6.

The reference section contains the full details:
Murphy, P.L. (2015), *Birds, Bees and Butterflies* (Garden Press, London).

Vancouver system Most commonly used in scientific journals. Each publication is numbered and the text reference is a superscript number. For example:
The variety of wildlife in our gardens[15] is amazing ...

The reference section contains the full details:
15. Murphy, P.L., *Birds, Bees and Butterflies* (London: Garden Press, 2015).

Note that any addition or subtraction from the list means that all subsequent items and the references will have to be renumbered.

author–title system Also known as the short-title system. A full reference is given only on the first mention in the chapter (or book if there is a bibliography).
    This is mostly for academic works. The whole title is cited in the first footnote, for example P.H. Clarke, *Visions of Utopia*, at which point you put, "hereafter Clarke, *Utopia*". Then on subsequent references you simply write "Clarke, *Utopia*", with page numbers if you wish.

mixed system Another system is common in academic publications. A superscript number is inserted in the text that corresponds with the number of a footnote (at the bottom of the page) or endnote (at the end of the chapter or the book). Footnotes and endnotes may be numbered by chapter or by book. The footnote or endnote consists of the bibliographical reference in full if there is no reference section or bibliography, or an abbreviated reference if there is. Sometimes the bibliographical reference appears in full on the first occurrence and is abbreviated subsequently, even if there is a reference section or bibliography.

Notes

- ibid. (abbreviation of *ibidem*, in the same place), not italic, is used to mean that the quote comes from the same source.

- op. cit. (abbreviation of *opere citato*, in the work quoted), not italic, is used to mean that the source has already been given.

Fractions

Do not mix fractions with decimals. If you need to convert one to the other, use this table. *See also* **figures** in Part 1.

Fraction	Decimal equivalent	Fraction	Decimal equivalent
$\frac{1}{2}$	0.5	$\frac{1}{12}$	0.083
$\frac{1}{3}$	0.333	$\frac{1}{13}$	0.077
$\frac{1}{4}$	0.25	$\frac{1}{14}$	0.071
$\frac{1}{5}$	0.2	$\frac{1}{15}$	0.067
$\frac{1}{6}$	0.167	$\frac{1}{16}$	0.063
$\frac{1}{7}$	0.143	$\frac{1}{17}$	0.059
$\frac{1}{8}$	0.125	$\frac{1}{18}$	0.056
$\frac{1}{9}$	0.111	$\frac{1}{19}$	0.053
$\frac{1}{10}$	0.1	$\frac{1}{20}$	0.05
$\frac{1}{11}$	0.091		

Geological eras

Astronomers and geologists give this broad outline of the ages of the universe and the earth.

Era, period and epoch	Years ago (m)	Characteristics
Origin of the universe (estimates vary markedly)	20,000–10,000	
Origin of the sun	5,000	
Origin of the earth	4,600	
Pre-Cambrian		
Archean	4,000	First signs of fossilised microbes
Proterozoic	2,500	
Palaeozoic		
Cambrian	570	First appearance of abundant fossils
Ordovician (obsolete)	500	Vertebrates emerge
Silurian	440	Fishes emerge
Devonian	400	Primitive plants emerge; age of fishes
Carboniferous	350	Amphibians emerge; first winged insects
Permian	270	Reptiles emerge
Mesozoic		
Triassic	250	Seed plants emerge
Jurassic	210	Age of dinosaurs
Cretaceous	145	Flowering plants emerge; dinosaurs extinct at end of this period

Cenozoic

Palaeocene		65	
Tertiary:	Eocene	55	Mammals emerge
	Oligocene	40	
	Miocene	25	
	Pliocene	5	
Quaternary:	Pleistocene	2	Ice ages; Stone Age man emerges
	Holocene or Recent	c. 11,000[a]	Modern man emerges

a   10,000 years, not 10,000m years.

Greek alphabet

These are the letters of the Greek alphabet and their names. The first column gives the upper-case symbol and the second column the lower-case symbol in each case.

A	α	alpha		N	ν	nu
B	β	beta		Ξ	ξ	xi
Γ	γ	gamma		O	o	omicron
Δ	δ	delta		Π	π	pi
E	ε	epsilon		P	ρ	rho
Z	ζ	zeta		Σ	ς or σ	sigma
H	η	eta		T	τ	tau
Θ	θ	theta		Υ	υ	upsilon
I	ι	iota		Φ	φ	phi
K	κ	kappa		X	χ	chi
Λ	λ	lambda		Ψ	ψ	psi
M	μ	mu		Ω	ω	omega

Latin

Here are some common Latin words and phrases, together with their translations.

ab initio	from the beginning
ad hoc	for this object or purpose (implied and "this one only"); therefore, without a system, spontaneously
ad hominem	to the man; used of an argument addressed to the presumed character or personal failings of the person on the other side
ad infinitum	to infinity, that is, endlessly
ad lib., ad libitum	at pleasure. Used adverbially to mean generously to the point of profligacy; as a verb, to invent or extemporise
ad nauseam	to a sickening extent
ad valorem	according to value (as opposed to volume)
a fortiori	with stronger reason
annus mirabilis	wonderful year, used to describe a year in which more than one memorable thing has happened; for instance 1666, the year of the Great Fire of London and the English defeats of the Dutch
a priori	from cause to effect, that is, deductively or from a pre-existing principle
bona fide	in good faith
carpe diem	literally pluck the day, but seize the day is more common; enjoy the moment; make the most of life
casus belli	the cause of (more often, pretext for) war

cave!	"Watch out!" (imperative); once used at boys' private schools in Britain
caveat emptor	let the buyer beware
ceteris paribus	other things being equal
cf	short for confer, meaning compare (imperative)
circa	around or about: used for dates and large quantities; can be abbreviated to c or c.
de facto	in point of fact, in effect
de jure	from the law; by right
de minimis	abbreviation of *de minimis non curat lex*, meaning the law is not concerned with trivial matters; too small to be taken seriously
de profundis	out of the depths
deus ex machina	God from a machine; first used of a Greek theatrical convention, where a god would swing on to the stage, high up in a machine, solving problems humans could not untangle and thus resolving the action of a play. Now used to describe a person or thing appearing from nowhere to put matters right
eg, exempli gratia	for example
et al., et alii	and others, used as an abbreviation in bibliographies when citing multiple editorship or authorship to save the writer the bother of writing out all the names. Thus, A. Bloggs *et al., The Occurrence of Endangered Species in the Genus Orthodoptera*
ex ante	before the event
ex cathedra	from the chair of office, authoritatively
ex gratia	as a favour, not under any compulsion
ex officio	by virtue of one's office, not unofficially
ex parte	from or for one side only
ex post facto, ex post	after the fact, retrospectively
ex tempore	off the cuff, without preparation (extempore)
habeas corpus	you must have the body; a writ to bring a person before a court, in most cases to ensure that the person's imprisonment is not illegal

horror vacui	literally, "fear of empty space"; the compulsion to make marks in every space. *Horror vacui* is indicated by a crowded design
ibid., ibidem	in the same place; used in footnotes in academic works to mean that the quote comes from the same source
idem	the same, as mentioned before; like ibidem
ie, id est	that is, explains the material immediately in front of it
in absentia	in the absence of, used as "absent"
in camera	in a (private) room, that is, not in public
in flagrante delicto	in the act of committing a crime; caught red-handed; an expression that has developed a sexual connotation
in loco	in the place of; eg, in loco parentis, in the place of a parent
in re	in the matter of
in situ	in (its) original place
inter alia/inter alios	among other things or people
intra vires	within the permitted powers (contrast with ultra vires)
ipso facto	by that very fact, in the fact itself
lingua franca	a common tongue
loc. cit., loco citato	in the place cited; used in footnotes to mean that the source of the reference or quote has already been given
mea culpa	my fault (commonly used as a noun while retaining the *mea*; eg, this *mea culpa* somewhat mollified them)
memento mori	remember you have to die; a reminder of death, such as a skull
mirabile dictu	literally, wonderful to relate
mutatis mutandis	things change and we must change with them; used to indicate making necessary changes over time
nem. con., nemine contradicente	no one against; unanimously

non sequitur	it does not follow; an inference or conclusion that does not follow from its premises
op. cit., opere citato	in the work quoted; similar to loc. cit. (see above)
pace	with due respect to
pari passu	on the same terms, at an equal pace or rate of progress
passim	adverb, here and there or scattered. Used in indexes to indicate that the item is scattered throughout the work and there are too many instances to enumerate them all
per se	by itself, for its own sake
persona non grata	person not in favour/barred
per stirpes	among families; a lawyer's term used when distributing an inheritance
petitio elenchis	the sin of assuming a conclusion
post eventum	after the event
post hoc, ergo propter hoc	after this, therefore because of this. Used fallaciously in argument to show that because one thing comes after another it can be inferred that the first thing caused the second thing
post mortem	after death, used as an adjective and also as a noun, a clinical examination of a dead body
prima facie	from a first impression, apparently at first sight, on the face of it – no connection with love
primus inter pares	first among equals
pro rata	for the rate; divided in proportion
pro tem., pro tempore	for the moment
PS, post scriptum	written afterwards
quid pro quo	something for something (or one thing for another), something in return, an equivalent
q.v., quod vide	which see; means that the reader should look for the word just mentioned (eg, in glossary)
re	with regard to, in the matter of
sic	thus; used in square brackets in quotes to show writer has made a mistake. "Mrs Thacher [sic] resigned today."

sine die	without (setting) a date
sine qua non	without which, not. Anything indispensable, and without which another cannot exist
status quo ante	the same state as before; usually shortened to status quo. A common usage is "maintaining the status quo"
stet	let it stand or do not delete; cancels an alteration in proofreading; dots are placed under what is to remain
sub judice	under judgment or consideration; not yet decided
sub rosa	under the rose, privately or furtively; not the same as under the gooseberry bush
ultra vires	beyond (one's) legal power
vade mecum	a little book or object carried about on the person; literally "Go with me"
vae victis	Woe to the conquered!
versus, v or v.	against; used in legal cases and games
viz, videlicet	that is to say; to wit; namely

Laws

Scientific, economic, facetious and fatalistic laws in common use are listed here.

Benford's law In lists of numbers from many sources of data the leading digit 1 occurs much more often than the others (about 30% of the time). The law was discovered by Simon Newcomb, an American astronomer, in 1881. He noted that the first pages of books of logarithms were much more thumbed than others. Furthermore, the higher the digit, the less likely it is to occur. This applies to mathematical constants as much as utility bills, addresses, share prices, birth and death statistics, the height of mountains, and so on.

Boyle's law The pressure of a gas varies inversely with its volume at constant temperature.

Brooks's law "Adding manpower to a late software project makes it later," said Fred Brooks, in his book *The Mythical Man-Month*.

Engel's law In general people spend a smaller share of their budget on food as their income increases.

Goodhart's law "Any observed statistical regularity will tend to collapse once pressure is placed upon it for control purposes" was the law stated by Charles Goodhart, a chief adviser to the Bank of England during the 1980s. It has been recast more succinctly as "When a measure becomes a target, it ceases to be a good measure."

Gresham's law When money of a high intrinsic value is in circulation with money of lesser value, it is the inferior currency which tends to remain in circulation, while the other is either hoarded or exported. In other words: "Bad money drives out good."

Heisenberg's uncertainty principle Energy and time or position and momentum cannot both be accurately measured simultaneously. The product of their uncertainties is h (Planck's constant).

Hooke's law The stress imposed on a solid is directly proportional to the strain produced within the elastic limit.

Laws of thermodynamics
1 The change in the internal energy of a system equals the sum of the heat added to the system and the work done on it.
2 Heat cannot be transferred from a colder to a hotter body within a system without net changes occurring in other bodies in the system.
3 It is impossible to reduce the temperature of a system to absolute zero in a finite number of steps.

Mendel's principles The law of segregation is that every somatic cell of an individual carries a pair of hereditary units for each character; the pairs separate during meiosis so that each gamete carries one unit only of each pair.

The law of independent assortment is that the separation of units of each pair is not influenced by that of any other pair.

Moore's law "The number of transistors on a chip doubles every 18–24 months." An observation by Gordon Moore, a founder of Intel, regarding the pace of semiconductor technology development in 1961.

Murphy's law Anything that can go wrong will go wrong. Also known as sod's law.

Ohm's law Electric current is directly proportional to electromotive force and inversely proportional to resistance.

Okun's law The relationship between unemployment and GDP growth. GDP growth of 3% will leave the jobless rate unchanged. Faster growth will cut the unemployment rate by half the amount by which growth exceeds 3%. A growth rate of less than 3% will increase unemployment by the same ratio.

Pareto principle Also known as the 80/20 rule, named after Vilfredo Pareto (1848–1923), an Italian economist, who determined that 80% of activity comes from 20% of the people. The principle was extended (or simply misunderstood) by Joseph Juran, an American management guru, who suggested that for many phenomena 80% of consequences stem from 20% of the causes. That is, in many instances a large number of results stem from a small number of causes, eg, 80% of problems come from 20% of the equipment or workforce.

Parkinson's law "Work expands so as to fill the time available for its completion." Formulated by C. Northcote Parkinson and first published in *The Economist*, November 19th 1955.

Parkinson's law of data Data expand to fill the space available for storage, so acquiring more memory will encourage the adoption of techniques that require more memory.

The Peter principle All members of a hierarchy rise to their own level of incompetence, according to Laurence Peter and Raymond Hull in their book of the same name published in 1969.

Reilly's law This law of retail gravitation suggests that people are generally attracted to the largest shopping centre in the area. William Reilly, an American academic, proposed the law in a book published in 1931.

Say's law of markets Aggregate supply creates its own aggregate demand. Attributed to Jean-Baptiste Say (1767–1832), a French economist. If output increases in a free-market economy, the sales would give the producers of the goods the same amount of income which would re-enter the economy and create demand for those goods. Keynes's law, attributed to John Maynard Keynes (1883–1946), a British economist, says that the opposite is true and that "demand creates its own supply" as businesses produce more to satisfy demand up to the limit of full employment.

sod's law See **Murphy's law.**

Utz's laws of computer programming Any given program, when running, is obsolete. If a program is useful, it will have to be changed. Any given program will expand to fill all available memory.

Wolfe's law of journalism
You cannot hope
to bribe or twist,
thank God! the
British journalist.

But seeing what
the man will do
unbribed, there's
no occasion to.

Mathematical symbols

+	plus or positive	$\gg$	much greater than
−	minus or negative	$\ll$	much less than
±	plus or minus, positive or negative	$\propto$	is proportional to or varies with
×	multiplied by	$\sqrt{}$	square root
÷ or /	divided by	$^r\sqrt{}$	rth root
=	equal to	r^n	r to the power of n
≡	identically equal to	$r!$ or ⌐r	factorial r
≠	not equal to	∞	infinity
≢	not identically equal to	%	per cent
≈ or ≅	approximately equal to, of the order of or similar to	‰	per mile (thousand)
∼		Σ	sum of
>	greater than	Π	product of
<	less than	Λ	difference
≯	not greater than	∴	therefore
≮	not less than		
≥	equal to or greater than		
≤	equal to or less than		

Measures

UK imperial units

The following imperial units are still used in the United Kingdom despite general conversion to the metric system: mile, yard, foot, inch for road traffic signs, distance and speed measurement; pint for draught beer and cider and for milk in returnable containers;

acre for land registration; troy ounce for transactions in precious metals; pounds and ounces in all small-scale (especially market) transactions involving weight.

Conversions

Acceleration

Standard gravity	=	10 metres (m) per second squared
	=	32 feet (ft) per second squared

Volume and capacity

5 millilitres	=	1 teaspoonful
26 UK fluid oz	=	25 US liquid oz
$1^3/_4$ UK pints	=	1 litre (l)
5 UK pints	=	6 US liquid pints
9 US liquid pints	=	9l
5 UK gallons	=	6 US gallons
1 US gallon	=	$3^3/_4$l
3 cubic (cu.) ft	=	85 cu. decimetres
	=	85l
$27^1/_2$ UK bushels	=	1 cu. m
$28^1/_3$ US bushels	=	1 cu. m
11 UK bushels	=	4 hectolitres
14 US bushels	=	5 hectolitres
1 US bushel (heaped)	=	$1^1/_4$ US bushels (struck)
1 US dry barrel	=	$3^1/_4$ US bushels
1 US cranberry barrel	=	$2^3/_4$ bushels
1 barrel (petroleum)	=	42 US gallons
	=	35 UK gallons
1 barrel per day	=	50 tonnes per year

Weight

1 grain	=	65 milligrams
15 grains	=	1 gram (g)
11 ounces (oz)	=	10 oz troy
1 ounce	=	28g
1 oz troy	=	31g
1 pound (lb)	=	454g
35 oz	=	1 kilogram (kg)

$$2\tfrac{1}{4}\text{lb} \;=\; 1\text{kg}$$
$$11 \text{ US tons} \;=\; 10 \text{ tonnes}$$
$$62 \text{ UK tons} \;=\; 63 \text{ tonnes}$$
$$100 \text{ UK (long) tons} \;=\; 112 \text{ US (short) tons}$$

Gold

The purity of gold is expressed as parts of 1,000, so that a fineness of 800 is 80% gold. Pure gold is defined as 24 carats (1,000 fine). Dental gold is usually 16 or 20 carat; gold in jewellery 9–22 carat. A golden sovereign is 22 carat.

1 metric carat = 200 milligrams.

Gold and silver are usually measured in troy weights: 1 troy ounce = 155.52 metric carats.

A standard international bar of gold is 400 troy ounces; bars of 250 troy ounces are also used.

Metric units

Metric units not generally recommended as SI units or for use with SI are marked with an asterisk (eg, Calorie*).

Length

10 angstroms =	1 nanometre
1,000 nanometres =	1 micrometre
1,000 micrometres =	1 millimetre (mm)
10mm =	1 centimetre (cm)
10cm =	1 decimetre
1,000mm =	1 metre (m)
100cm =	1m
10 decimetres =	1m
100m =	1 hectometre
10 hectometres =	1 kilometre (km)
1,000km =	1 megametre
nautical: 1,852m =	1 int. nautical mile

Area

100 sq. mm	=	1 sq. cm
100 sq. cm	=	1 sq. decimetre
100 sq. decimetres	=	1 sq. m
100 sq. m	=	1 are
10,000 sq. m	=	1 hectare (ha)
100 ares	=	1 ha
100 ha	=	1 sq. kilometre

Weight (mass)

1,000 milligrams (mg)	=	1 gram (g)
1,000g	=	1 kilogram (kg)
100kg	=	1 quintal
1,000kg	=	1 tonne

Volume

1,000 cu. mm	=	1 cu. cm
1,000 cu. cm	=	1 cu. decimetre
1,000 cu. decimetres	=	1 cu. m

Capacity

10 millilitres (ml)	=	1 centilitre (cl)
10cl	=	1 decilitre (dl)
10dl	=	1 litre (l)
1 litre	=	1 cu. decimetre
100 litres	=	1hl
1,000l	=	1 kilolitre
10 hectolitres	=	1 kilolitre
1 kilolitre	=	1 cu. metre

Metric system prefixes

Prefix	Symbol	Factor by which unit is multiplied		Description
atto	a	10^{-18} =	0.000 000 000 000 000 001	
femto	f	10^{-15} =	0.000 000 000 000 001	
pico	p	10^{-12} =	0.000 000 000 001	million millionth; trillionth
nano	n	10^{-9} =	0.000 000 001	thousand millionth; billionth
micro	μ	10^{-6} =	0.000 001	millionth

milli	m	10^{-3}	=	0.001	thousandth
centi	c	10^{-2}	=	0.01	hundredth
deci	d	10^{-1}	=	0.1	tenth
deca (or deka)	da[a]	10^{1}	=	10	ten
hecto	h	10^{2}	=	100	hundred
kilo	k	10^{3}	=	1,000	thousand
myria	my	10^{4}	=	10,000	ten thousand
mega	M	10^{6}	=	1,000,000	million
giga	G	10^{9}	=	1,000,000,000	thousand million; billion
tera	T	10^{12}	=	1,000,000,000,000	million million; trillion
peta	P	10^{15}	=	1,000,000,000,000,000	
exa	E	10^{18}	=	1,000,000,000,000,000,000	

a Sometimes dk is used (eg, in Germany).

Miscellaneous units and ratios

Beer

small	=	half pint
large	=	1 pint
flagon	=	1 quart
anker	=	10 gallons

Champagne

2 bottles	=	1 magnum
4 bottles	=	1 jeroboam
20 bottles	=	1 nebuchadnezzar

Wines and spirits

	Proof (Sikes) (°)	Volume of alcohol (%)
Table wines	14-26	8-15
Port, sherry	26-38.5	15-22
Whisky, gin	65.5-70	37.5-40

tot (whisky, gin, rum or vodka) = 25ml or 35ml (before end-1994, one-sixth to one-quarter gill; the larger size is mainly used in Scotland)

wine glass	=	125ml or 175ml
wine bottle or carafe (metric sizes)	=	25cl, 50cl, 75cl or 1l

Precious metals

1 metric carat	=	200mg
1 troy oz	=	155.52 metric carats

Water

1 litre weighs 1kg.
1 cubic m weighs 1 tonne.
1 UK gallon weighs 10.022lb.
1 US gallon weighs 8.345lb.

Energy

1 therm	=	29.3071 kilowatt hours (kW h)
1 terawatt hour (TW h)	=	1 thousand million kilowatt hours
1 watt second	=	1 joule
1 kilowatt hour	=	36 megajoules (MJ)
1 calorie (dieticians')	=	4.1855 kilojoules

Radioactivity

1 becquerel (Bq)	=	1 disintegration per sec.
1 rutherford	=	1m Bq

Dose of radiation

1 rad	=	10 millijoules per kg
1 gray	=	100 rad = 1 joule per kg
1 rem	=	1 rad, weighted by radiation effect
1 sievert (Sv)	=	100 rems
Background dose (UK)	=	25 millisievert (mSv) per year

Energy is measured in kilowatt hours and power is measured in kilowatts. Energy is power multiplied by time, thus the kilowatt-hour is one unit of energy.

Crude oil

1 barrel	=	42 US gallons
	=	34.97 UK (imperial) gallons
	=	0.159 cubic m (159l)
	=	0.136 tonne (approx.)
1 barrel per day (b/d)	=	50 tonnes per year (approx.)

Clothing sizes (rough equivalents)

Men's suits

UK/US	32	34	36	38	40	42	44
Europe	42	44	46	48	50	52	54
Metric	81	86	91	97	102	107	112

Women's suits, dresses, skirts

UK	10	12	14	16	18	20	22
US	8	10	12	14	16	18	20
Europe	38	40	42	44	47	50	52

Men's shirts (collar sizes)

UK/US (in)	15	15.5	16	16.5	17	17.5
Europe (cm)	38	39.5	41	42	43	44

Shoes

UK	5	6	7	8	9	10
US men's	6	7	8	9	10	11
US women's	6.5	7.5	8.5	9.5	10.5	11.5
Europe	38	39	40.5	42	43	44.5

Paper sizes

"A" Series (metric sizes)

A0 = 841mm × 1,189mm (33.11 in × 46.81 in)
A3 = 297mm × 420mm (11.69 in × 16.54 in)
A4 = 210mm × 297mm (8.27 in × 11.69 in)
A5 = 148mm × 210mm (5.83 in × 8.27 in)
A6 = 105mm × 148mm (4.13 in × 5.83 in)
A7 = 74mm × 105mm (2.91 in × 4.13 in)

Conversion factors[a]

Multiply number of	by	to obtain equivalent number of
Length		
inches (in)	25.4	millimetres (mm)
inches	2.54	centimetres (cm)
feet (ft)	30.48	centimetres
feet	0.3048	metres (m)
yards (yd)	0.9144	metres
miles (land 5,280 ft)	1.609344	kilometres (km)
miles (UK sea)	1.853184	kilometres
miles, international nautical	1.852	kilometres
Area		
sq. inches (in^2)	645.16	sq. millimetres (mm^2)
sq. inches	6.4516	sq. centimetres (cm^2)
sq. ft (ft^2)	929.0304	sq. centimetres
sq. ft	0.092903	sq. metres (m^2)
sq. yards (yd^2)	0.836127	sq. metres
acres	4046.86	sq. metres
acres	0.404686	hectares (ha)
acres	0.004047	sq. kilometres (km^2)
sq. miles	2.58999	sq. kilometres
Volume and capacity		
cu. inches (in^3)	16.387064	cu. centimetres (cm^3)
UK pints	34.6774	cu. inches
UK pints	0.5683	litres (l)
UK gallons	4.54609	litres
US gallons	3.785	litres
cu. feet (ft^3)	28.317	litres
cu. feet	0.028317	cu. metres (cm^3)
UK gallons	1.20095	US gallons

Multiply number of	by	to obtain equivalent number of
Length		
millimetres	0.03937	inches
centimetres	0.3937	inches
centimetres	0.03281	feet
metres	39.3701	inches
metres	3.2808	feet
metres	1.0936	yards
metres	0.54681	fathoms
kilometres	0.62137	miles (land)
kilometres	0.53961	miles (UK sea)
kilometres	0.53996	miles, international nautical
Area		
sq. millimetres	0.00155	sq. inches
sq. centimetres	0.1550	sq. inches
sq. metres	10.7639	sq. feet
sq. metres	1.19599	sq. yards
hectares	2.47105	acres
sq. kilometres	247.105	acres
sq. kilometres	0.3861	sq. miles
Volume and capacity		
cu. centimetres	0.06102	cu. inches
litres	61.024	cu. inches
litres	2.1134	US pints
litres	1.7598	UK pints
litres	0.2642	US gallons
litres	0.21997	UK gallons
hectolitres	26.417	US gallons
hectolitres	21.997	UK gallons

Multiply number of	by	to obtain equivalent number of
US gallons	0.832674	UK gallons

Weight (mass)

ounces, avoirdupois (oz)	28.3495	grams (g)
ounces, troy (oz tr)	31.1035	grams
ounces, avoirdupois	0.9115	ounces, troy
pounds, avoirdupois (lb)	453.59237	grams
pounds, avoirdupois (lb)	0.45359	kilograms (kg)
short tons (2,000 lb)	0.892857	long tons
short tons (2,000 lb)	0.907185	tonnes (t)
long tons (2,240 lb)	1.12	short tons
long tons (2,240 lb)	1.01605	tonnes

Velocity and fuel consumption

miles/hour	1.609344	kilometres/hour
miles/hour	0.868976	international knots
miles/UK gallon	0.35401	kilometres/litre
miles/US gallon	0.42514	kilometres/litre
UK gallons/mile[b]	282.481	litres/100 kilometres
US gallons/mile[b]	235.215	litres/100 kilometres

Temperature

degrees Fahrenheit	5/9 after subtracting 32	degrees Celsius (centigrade)
−40°F	equals	−40°C
32°F	equals	0°C
59°F	equals	15°C

a Between the UK and US systems, and the International System of Units (SI). As an example of the use of the table, 10 long tons (of 2,240lb each), multiplied by 1.12, is equal to 11.2 short tons (of 2,000lb each).

Multiply number of	by	to obtain equivalent number of
hectolitres	2.838	US bushels
hectolitres	2.750	UK bushels
cu. metres	35.3147	cu. feet
cu. metres	1.30795	cu. yards
cu. metres	264.172	US gallons

Weight (mass)

grams	0.03527	ounces, avoirdupois
grams	0.03215	ounces, troy
kilograms	2.20462	pounds, avoirdupois
metric quintals (q)	220.462	pounds, avoirdupois
tonnes	2,204.62	pounds, avoirdupois
tonnes	1.10231	short tons
tonnes	0.984207	long tons

Velocity and fuel consumption

kilometres/hour	0.62137	miles/hour
kilometres/hour	0.53996	international knots
kilometres/litre	2.82481	miles/UK gallon
litres/100 kilometres[c]	0.00354	UK gallons/mile
litres/100 kilometres[c]	0.00425	US gallons/mile

Temperature

degrees Celsius	9/5 and add 32	degrees Fahrenheit
37°C	equals	98.6°F
50°C	equals	122°F
100°C	equals	212°F

b Miles per UK gallon, divided into 282.481, gives litres per 100 kilometres; miles per US gallon, divided into 235.215, gives litres per 100 kilometres.

c Litres per 100 kilometres, divided into 282.481, gives miles per UK gallon; litres per 100 kilometres, divided into 235.215, gives miles per US gallon.

National accounts

These are the definitions adopted by the United Nations in 1968.
See http://unstats.un.org/unsd/nationalaccount/ for more details.

Final expenditure

= private final consumption expenditure ("consumers' expenditure")
+ government final consumption expenditure
+ increase in stocks
+ gross fixed capital formation
+ exports of goods and services

Gross domestic product (GDP) at market prices

= final expenditure
− imports of goods and services

Gross national income or product (GNI/GNP) at market prices

= gross domestic product at market prices
+ net income from other countries

Gross domestic product at factor cost

= gross domestic product at market prices
− indirect taxes
+ subsidies

North America administrative divisions

Here are the main administrative subdivisions of the United States and Canada. *See also* **countries and their inhabitants, placenames** in Part 1.

United States

States

Alabama (AL)	Montana (MT)
Alaska (AK)	Nebraska (NE)
Arizona (AZ)	Nevada (NV)
Arkansas (AR)	New Hampshire (NH)
California (CA)	New Jersey (NJ)
Colorado (CO)	New Mexico (NM)
Connecticut (CT)	New York (NY)
Delaware (DE)	North Carolina (NC)
District of Columbia (DC)[a]	North Dakota (ND)
Florida (FL)	Ohio (OH)
Georgia (GA)	Oklahoma (OK)
Hawaii (HI)	Oregon (OR)
Idaho (ID)	Pennsylvania (PA)
Illinois (IL)	Puerto Rico (PR)
Indiana (IN)	Rhode Island (RI)
Iowa (IA)	South Carolina (SC)
Kansas (KS)	South Dakota (SD)
Kentucky (KY)	Tennessee (TN)
Louisiana (LA)	Texas (TX)
Maine (ME)	Utah (UT)
Maryland (MD)	Vermont (VT)
Massachusetts (MA)	Virginia (VA)
Michigan (MI)	Washington (WA)
Minnesota (MN)	West Virginia (WV)
Mississippi (MS)	Wisconsin (WI)
Missouri (MO)	Wyoming (WY)

a   DC is not a state.

Canada

Provinces

Alberta	Manitoba
British Columbia	New Brunswick

Newfoundland and Labrador
Nova Scotia
Ontario

Prince Edward Island
Quebec (Québec)
Saskatchewan

Territories
Northwest Territories
Nunavut

Yukon

Olympic games

Summer

I	Athens	1896	XVII	Rome	1960
II	Paris	1900	XVIII	Tokyo	1964
III	St Louis	1904	XIX	Mexico City	1968
IV	London	1908	XX	Munich	1972
V	Stockholm	1912	XXI	Montreal	1976
VI	Berlin (cancelled)	1916	XXII	Moscow	1980
VII	Antwerp	1920	XXIII	Los Angeles	1984
VIII	Paris	1924	XXIV	Seoul	1988
IX	Amsterdam	1928	XXV	Barcelona	1992
X	Los Angeles	1932	XXVI	Atlanta	1996
XI	Berlin	1936	XXVII	Sydney	2000
			XXVIII	Athens	2004
XII	Tokyo/Helsinki (cancelled)	1940	XXIX	Beijing	2008
XIII	London (cancelled)	1944	XXX	London	2012
XIV	London	1948	XXXI	Rio de Janeiro	2016
XV	Helsinki	1952	XXXII	Tokyo	2020
XVI	Melbourne	1956			

Winter

I	Chamonix, France	1924	IV	Garmisch-Partenkirchen, Germany	1936
II	St Moritz, Switzerland	1928		Cancelled	1940
III	Lake Placid, United States	1932		Cancelled	1944

V	St Moritz, Switzerland	1948	**XV**	Calgary, Canada	1988
VI	Oslo, Norway	1952	**XVI**	Albertville, France	1992[a]
VII	Cortina d'Ampezzo, Italy	1956	**XVII**	Lillehammer, Norway	1994[a]
VIII	Squaw Valley, United States	1960	**XVIII**	Nagano, Japan	1998
IX	Innsbruck, Austria	1964	**XIX**	Salt Lake City, United States	2002
X	Grenoble, France	1968	**XX**	Torino (Turin), Italy	2006
XI	Sapporo, Japan	1972	**XXI**	Vancouver, Canada	2010
XII	Innsbruck, Austria	1976	**XXII**	Sochi, Russia	2014
XIII	Lake Placid, United States	1980	**XXIII**	Pyongchang, South Korea	2018
XIV	Sarajevo, Yugoslavia	1984			

a Since 1994 the summer and winter Olympic games have taken place in alternate even-numbered years. Hence, the Albertville and Lillehammer winter games are only two years apart.

Organisations

These are the exact names and abbreviated titles of the main international organisations. Where membership is small or exclusive, members are listed too.

African Union formerly the Organisation of African Unity (OAU), founded in 1963, headquarters in Addis Ababa, Ethiopia.

Members

Algeria	Central African	Eritrea
Angola	Republic	Ethiopia
Benin	Chad	Gabon
Botswana	Comoros	The Gambia
Burkina Faso	Congo-Brazzaville	Ghana
Burundi	Djibouti	Guinea
Cameroon	Egypt	Guinea-
Cape Verde	Equatorial Guinea	Bissau

Ivory Coast	Mozambique	Somalia
Kenya	Namibia	South Africa
Lesotho	Niger	South Sudan
Liberia	Nigeria	Sudan
Libya	Rwanda	Swaziland
Madagascar	São Tomé and	Tanzania
Malawi	Principe	Togo
Mali	Senegal	Uganda
Mauritania	Seychelles	
Mauritius	Sierra Leone	

ALADI Asociación Latinoamericana de Integración (Latin American Integration Association), founded in 1980, based in Montevideo, Uruguay.

Members[a]

Argentina	Cuba	Peru
Bolivia	Ecuador	Uruguay
Brazil	Mexico	Venezuela
Chile	Panama	
Colombia	Paraguay	

a There are also 17 observer countries and 10 observer organisations.

Andean Community of Nations founded in 1969, headquarters in Lima, Peru.

Members

| Bolivia | Ecuador |
| Colombia | Peru |

APEC Asia-Pacific Economic Cooperation, founded in 1989, based in Singapore.

Members

Australia	Hong Kong, China	Peru
Brunei Darussalam	Indonesia	Philippines
Canada	Japan	Russia
Chile	Malaysia	Singapore
China	Mexico	Thailand
Chinese Taipei	New Zealand	United States
(Taiwan)	Papua New Guinea	Vietnam

ASEAN Association of Southeast Asian Nations, established in 1967, headquarters in Jakarta, Indonesia.

Members

Brunei Darussalam	Malaysia	Thailand
Cambodia	Myanmar	Vietnam
Indonesia	Philippines	
Laos	Singapore	

BIS Bank for International Settlements, the central bankers' central bank, founded 1930, based in Basel, Switzerland.

Members[a]

Algeria	Greece	Philippines
Argentina	Hong Kong	Poland
Australia	Hungary	Portugal
Austria	Iceland	Romania
Belgium	India	Russia
Bosnia &	Indonesia	Saudi Arabia
Herzegovina	Ireland	Serbia
Brazil	Israel	Singapore
Bulgaria	Italy	Slovakia
Canada	Japan	Slovenia
Chile	Latvia	South Africa
China	Lithuania	South Korea
Colombia	Luxembourg	Spain
Croatia	Macedonia	Sweden
Czech Republic	Malaysia	Switzerland
Denmark	Mexico	Thailand
Estonia	Netherlands	Turkey
Finland	New Zealand	United Arab Emirates
France	Norway	United Kingdom
Germany	Peru	United States

a The European Central Bank is a shareholder.

CARICOM Caribbean Community and Common Market, formed in 1973, secretariat in Georgetown, Guyana.

Members

Anguilla[a]	Antigua and Barbuda	Bahamas[b]

Barbados
Belize
Bermuda[a]
British Virgin
  Islands[a]
Cayman Islands[a]
Dominica

Grenada
Guyana
Haiti
Jamaica
Montserrat
St Kitts-Nevis
St Lucia

St Vincent and the
  Grenadines
Suriname
Trinidad and Tobago
Turks and Caicos
  Islands[a]

a Associate member.
b Member of the Community but not the Common Market.

COMESA Common Market for Eastern and Southern Africa, founded in 1994, headquarters in Lusaka, Zambia.

Members

Burundi
Comoros
Congo, Democratic
  Republic of
Djibouti
Egypt
Eritrea

Ethiopia
Kenya
Libya
Madagascar
Malawi
Mauritius
Rwanda

Seychelles
Sudan
Swaziland
Uganda
Zambia
Zimbabwe

Commonwealth based in London, UK.

Members

Antigua and Barbuda
Australia
Bahamas
Bangladesh
Barbados
Belize
Botswana
Brunei Darussalam
Cameroon
Canada
Cyprus
Dominica
Fiji Islands[a]
Ghana
Grenada

Guyana
India
Jamaica
Kenya
Kiribati
Lesotho
Malawi
Malaysia
Maldives
Malta
Mauritius
Mozambique
Namibia
Nauru[b]
New Zealand

Nigeria
Pakistan
Papua New Guinea
Rwanda
Samoa
Seychelles
Sierra Leone
Singapore
Solomon Islands
South Africa
Sri Lanka
St Kitts and Nevis
St Lucia
St Vincent and the
  Grenadines

Swaziland	Trinidad and Tobago	United Kingdom
Tanzania	Tuvalu	Vanuatu
Tonga	Uganda	Zambia

a Suspended on September 1st 2009.
b Member in arrears.

Dependencies and associated states

Australia

Ashmore and Cartier Islands	Coral Sea Islands Territory
Australian Antarctic Territory	Heard and McDonald Islands
Christmas Island	Norfolk Island
Cocos (Keeling) Islands	

New Zealand

| Cook Islands | Ross Dependency |
| Niue | Tokelau |

UK

Anguilla	Isle of Man
Bermuda	Montserrat
British Antarctic Territory	Pitcairn Island
British Indian Ocean Territory	South Georgia and South
British Virgin Islands	Sandwich Islands
Cayman Islands	St Helena, Ascension and Tristan
Channel Islands	da Cunha
Falkland Islands	Turks and Caicos Islands
Gibraltar	

Commonwealth of Independent States (CIS) founded by the former Soviet Socialist Republics in December 1991, based in Moscow, Russia.

Members

Armenia	Moldova
Azerbaijan	Russia
Belarus	Tajikistan
Georgia	Turkmenistan
Kazakhstan	Ukraine
Kyrgyzstan	Uzbekistan

ECOWAS Economic Community of West African States, founded 1975, secretariat in Abuja, Nigeria.

Members

Benin	Guinea-Bissau	Nigeria
Burkina Faso	Ivory Coast	Senegal
Cape Verde	Liberia	Sierra Leone
Ghana	Mali	The Gambia
Guinea	Niger	Togo

EEA European Economic Area, negotiated in 1992 between the European Community and members of EFTA, came into force in 1994 and has been maintained because the three signatories – Iceland, Norway and Liechtenstein – wanted to participate in the single market without being full members of the EU.

EFTA European Free Trade Association, established 1960.

Members

Iceland	Norway
Liechtenstein	Switzerland

Euro area Name given to the economic region formed by the EU member countries that have adopted the euro as their currency. Also known as the euro zone.

Members

Austria[a]	Greece (2001)	Netherlands[a]
Belgium[a]	Ireland[a]	Portugal[a]
Cyprus (2008)	Italy[a]	Slovakia (2009)
Estonia (2011)	Latvia (2014)	Slovenia (2007)
Finland[a]	Lithuania (2015)	Spain
France[a]	Luxembourg[a]	
Germany[a]	Malta (2008)	

a Joined in 1999 when the euro was introduced.

EU European Union, the collective designation of three organisations with common membership: the European Coal and Steel Community (ECSC, treaty expired in 2002), European Economic Community (EEC) and European Atomic Energy Community (EURATOM). They merged to become the European

Community (EC) in 1967. In November 1993 when the Maastricht treaty came into force the EC was incorporated into the EU. Economic and Monetary Union (EMU) formed one of the articles of the Maastricht treaty, in which were set out the stages by which the EU would progress to full convergence, with a single currency, the euro. Headquarters in Brussels, with some activities in Luxembourg and Strasbourg.

Main institutions

Council of the European Union   European Council
European Commission   European Parliament

Other EU institutions
Committee of the Regions
Computer Emergency Response Team (CERT)
Court of Auditors
Court of Justice of the EU
European Central Bank
European Data Protection Supervisor
European Economic and Social Committee
European External Action Service (EEAS)
European Investment Bank
European Investment Fund
European Ombudsman
European Personnel Selection Office
European School of Administration
Publications Office

Decentralised agencies
Agency for the Cooperation of Energy Regulators (ACER)
Body of European Regulators for Electronic Communications
    (BEREC)
Community Plant Variety Office (CPVO)
European Agency for Safety and Health at Work (EU-OSHA)
European Agency for the Management of Operational Cooperation
    at the External Borders (FRONTEX)
European Agency for the operational management of large-scale IT
    systems in the area of freedom, security and justice (EU-LISA)
European Asylum Support Office (EASO)
European Aviation Safety Agency (EASA)

European Banking Authority (EBA)
European Centre for Disease Prevention and Control (ECDC)
European Centre for the Development of Vocational Training
(CEDEFOP)
European Chemicals Agency (ECHA)
European Defence Agency (EDA)
European Environment Agency (EEA)
European Fisheries Control Agency (EFCA)
European Food Safety Authority (EFSA)
European Foundation for the Improvement of Living and Working
Conditions (EUROFOUND)
European GNSS Agency (GSA)
European Institute for Gender Equality (EIGE)
European Insurance and Occupational Pensions Authority (EIOPA)
European Maritime Safety Agency (EMSA)
European Medicines Agency (EMA)
European Monitoring Centre for Drugs and Drug Addiction
(EMCDDA)
European Network and Information Security Agency (ENISA)
European Police College (Cepol)
European Police Office (Europol)
European Public Prosecutor's Office (in preparation) (EPPO)
European Railway Agency (ERA)
European Securities and Markets Authority (ESMA)
European Training Foundation (ETF)
European Union Agency for Fundamental Rights (FRA)
European Union Institute for Security Studies (EUISS)
European Union Satellite Centre (EUSC)
Office for Harmonisation in the Internal Market (OHIM)
Single Resolution Board (in preparation) (SRB)
The European Union's Judicial Cooperation Unit (EUROJUST)
Translation Centre for the Bodies of the European Union (CdT)

Executive agencies
Consumers, Health and Food Executive Agency (CHAFEA)
Education, Audiovisual and Culture Executive Agency (EACEA)
European Research Council Executive Agency (ERC Executive
Agency)

Executive Agency for Small and Medium-sized Enterprises (EASME)
Innovation & Networks Executive Agency (INEA)
Research Executive Agency (REA)

Other EU agencies
European Atomic Energy Community Treaty (EURATOM)
European Institute of Innovation and Technology (EIT)

Members

Austria (1995)	France[a]	Netherlands[a]
Belgium[a]	Germany[a]	Poland (2004)
Bulgaria (2007)	Greece (1981)	Portugal (1986)
Croatia (2013)	Hungary (2004)	Romania (2007)
Cyprus (2004)	Ireland (1973)	Slovakia (2004)
Czech Republic	Italy[a]	Slovenia (2004)
(2004)	Latvia (2004)	Spain (1986)
Denmark (1973)	Lithuania (2004)	Sweden (1995)
Estonia (2004)	Luxembourg[a]	UK (1973)
Finland (1995)	Malta (2004)	

a Founding member.
Note: Year of joining in brackets.

FTAA Free Trade Area of the Americas, set up in November 2002 to integrate the economies of the western hemisphere into a single free trade agreement.

Members

Antigua & Barbuda	Ecuador	St Kitts & Nevis
Argentina	El Salvador	St Lucia
Bahamas	Grenada	St Vincent & the
Barbados	Guatemala	Grenadines
Belize	Guyana	Suriname
Bolivia	Haiti	Trinidad & Tobago
Brazil	Honduras	United States
Canada	Jamaica	Uruguay
Chile	Mexico	Venezuela
Colombia	Nicaragua	
Costa Rica	Panama	
Dominica	Paraguay	
Dominican Republic	Peru	

GCC Co-operation Council for the Arab States of the Gulf or Gulf Co-operation Council, established in 1981, headquarters in Riyadh, Saudi Arabia.

Members

Bahrain	Oman	Saudi Arabia
Kuwait	Qatar	United Arab Emirates

G7, G8, G10, G22, G26 In 1975, six countries, the world's leading capitalist countries, ranked by GDP, were represented in France at the first annual summit meeting: the United States, the UK, West Germany, Japan and Italy, as well as the host country. The following year they were joined by Canada and, in 1977, by representatives of the European Union, although the group continued to be known as the G7. At the 1989 summit, 15 developing countries were also represented, although this did not give birth to the G22, which was not set up until 1998 and swiftly grew into G26. At the 1991 G7 summit, a meeting was held with the Soviet Union, a practice that continued (with Russia) in later years. In 1997, although it was not one of the world's eight richest countries, Russia became a full member of the G8. It was excluded again, because of its actions in Crimea and Ukraine, in 2014. Meetings of the IMF are attended by the G10, which includes 11 countries.

G10 members

Belgium	Italy	Switzerland
Canada	Japan	United Kingdom
France	Netherlands	United States
Germany	Sweden	

IATA International Air Transport Association, head offices in Montreal and Geneva; regional offices in Miami and Singapore.

Members: most international airlines

International Seabed Authority an autonomous organisation in relationship with the UN, established 1994, based in Kingston, Jamaica

Members: 157 signatories to the Convention on the Law of the Sea.

Mercosur Mercado Común del Sur (Southern Common Market), founded in 1991, based in Montevideo, Uruguay.

Members	Associate members
Argentina	Bolivia
Brazil	Chile
Paraguay	Colombia
Suriname	Ecuador
Uruguay	Guyana
Venezuela	Peru

NAFTA North American Free Trade Agreement, which came into force on January 1st 1994.

Members

Canada	Mexico	United States

NATO North Atlantic Treaty Organisation, an alliance of 28 countries from Europe and North America committed to fulfilling goals of North Atlantic Treaty signed on April 4th 1949; headquarters in Brussels.

Members

Albania	Greece	Portugal
Belgium	Hungary	Romania
Bulgaria	Iceland	Slovakia
Canada	Italy	Slovenia
Croatia	Latvia	Spain
Czech Republic	Lithuania	Turkey
Denmark	Luxembourg	United Kingdom
Estonia	Netherlands	United States
France	Norway	
Germany	Poland	

OAS Organisation of American States, formed in 1948, headquarters in Washington, DC.

Members[a][b]

Antigua and Barbuda	Belize	Chile
Argentina	Bolivia	Colombia
Bahamas	Brazil	Costa Rica
Barbados	Canada	Dominica

Dominican Republic	Jamaica	St Vincent and the
Ecuador	Mexico	Grenadines
El Salvador	Nicaragua	Suriname
Grenada	Panama	Trinidad and Tobago
Guatemala	Paraguay	United States
Guyana	Peru	Uruguay
Haiti	St Kitts-Nevis	Venezuela
Honduras[c]	St Lucia	

a Has many permanent non-member observers.
b Cuba was excluded from the OAS in 1962. However, on June 3rd 2009 it was decided that the 1962 Resolution would no longer apply.
c Honduras was suspended from active participation on July 5th 2009.

OECD Organisation for Economic Co-operation and Development, capitalism's club, founded in 1961, based in Paris. The European Commission also takes part in the OECD's work.

Members

Australia	Hungary	Portugal
Austria	Iceland	Slovakia
Belgium	Ireland	Slovenia
Canada	Israel	South Korea
Chile	Italy	Spain
Czech Republic	Japan	Sweden
Denmark	Luxembourg	Switzerland
Estonia	Mexico	Turkey
Finland	Netherlands	United Kingdom
France	New Zealand	United States
Germany	Norway	
Greece	Poland	

OPEC Organisation of the Petroleum Exporting Countries, established 1960, based in Vienna.

Members

Algeria	Iraq	Qatar
Ecuador[a]	Kuwait	Saudi Arabia
Indonesia[b]	Libya	United Arab Emirates
Iran	Nigeria	Venezuela

a Ecuador suspended its membership between December 1992 and October 2007.
b Indonesia suspended its membership from January 2009.

OSCE Organisation for Security and Co-operation in Europe, originally founded in 1972 as the Conference on Security and Co-operation in Europe (CSCE).

Members: 57, including European countries, Canada, the US and former republics of the Soviet Union

SADC Southern African Development Community, replaced the Southern African Development Co-ordination Conference in 1992, based in Gaborone, Botswana. Its aim is to work for development and economic growth in the region with common systems and institutions, promoting peace and security, and achieving complementary national and regional strategies.

Members

Angola	Malawi	Swaziland
Botswana	Mauritius	Tanzania
Congo, Democratic	Mozambique	Zambia
Republic of	Namibia	Zimbabwe
Lesotho	Seychelles	
Madagascar	South Africa	

The United Nations (UN) officially came into existence on October 24th 1945, based in New York, US.

Main bodies

General Assembly	International Court of Justice
Security Council	Secretariat
Economic and Social Council (ECOSOC)	Repertory of Practice of United Nations Organs
Trusteeship Council	

Secretaries-general
Sir Gladwyn Jebb (UK), acting, 1945–46
Trygve Lie (Norway), February 1946 to his resignation in November 1952
Dag Hammarskjöld (Sweden), April 1953 until his death in a plane crash in Northern Rhodesia (now Zambia), September 1961
U Thant (Burma, now Myanmar), November 1961–December 1971
Kurt Waldheim (Austria) 1972–81
Javier Pérez de Cuéllar (Peru) 1982–91

Boutros Boutros-Ghali (Egypt), January 1992 to the American veto of
his second term in December 1996
Kofi Annan (Ghana), 1997–2006
Ban Ki-moon (South Korea), 2007–

Regional commissions		*Head office*
Economic Commission for Africa	ECA	Addis Ababa
Economic Commission for Europe	ECE	Geneva
Economic Commission for Latin America and the Caribbean	ECLAC	Santiago
Economic and Social Commission for Asia and the Pacific	ESCAP	Bangkok
Economic and Social Commission for Western Asia	ESCWA	Beirut

Other UN bodies and programmes		
Department of Peacekeeping Operations	DPKO	New York
International Trade Centre	ITC	Geneva
Office for the Co-ordination of Humanitarian Affairs	OCHA	New York
Office of United Nations High Commissioner for Human Rights	OHCHR	Geneva
United Nations Capital Development Fund	UNCDF	New York
United Nations Children's Fund	UNICEF	New York
United Nations Conference on Trade and Development	UNCTAD	Geneva
United Nations Development Programme	UNDP	New York
United Nations Environment Programme	UNEP	Nairobi
United Nations High Commissioner for Refugees	UNHCR	Geneva
United Nations Human Settlements Programme	UN-Habitat	Nairobi
United Nations Institute for Research and Training	UNITAR	Geneva
United Nations Office on Drugs and Crime	UNODC	Vienna
United Nations Population Fund	UNFPA	New York

United Nations Relief and Works Agency for Palestine Refugees in the Near East	UNRWA	Gaza City, Palestinian Territories
United Nations Volunteers	UNV	Bonn
United Nations Entity for Gender Equality and the Empowerment of Women	UN women	New York
World Food Programme	WFP	Rome

Specialised agencies within the UN system

Food and Agriculture Organisation	FAO	Rome
International Civil Aviation Organisation	ICAO	Montreal
International Fund for Agricultural Development	IFAD	Rome
International Labour Organisation	ILO	Geneva
International Maritime Organisation	IMO	London
International Monetary Fund	IMF	Washington, DC
International Telecommunication Union	ITU	Geneva
United Nations Educational, Scientific and Cultural Organisation	UNESCO	Paris
United Nations Industrial Development Organisation	UNIDO	Vienna
Universal Postal Union	UPU	Berne
World Bank Group[a]		Washington, DC
World Health Organisation	WHO	Geneva
World Intellectual Property Organisation	WIPO	Geneva
World Meteorological Organisation	WMO	Geneva
World Tourism Organisation	UNWTO	Madrid

a Comprising the International Bank for Reconstruction and Development (IBRD), the International Centre for Settlement of Investment Disputes (ICSID), the International Development Association (IDA), the International Finance Corporation (IFC), and the Multilateral Investment Guarantee Agency (MIGA).

Related organisations

International Atomic Energy Agency	IAEA	Vienna
Preparatory Commission for the Comprehensive Nuclear-Test-Ban Treaty Organisation	CTBTO	Vienna

Organisation for the Prohibition of   OPCW   The Hague
  Chemical Weapons

WTO World Trade Organisation, the international organisation
of the world trading system with co-operative links to the UN,
established in 1995 as successor to the General Agreement on Tariffs
and Trade (GATT), based in Geneva.

Members: 160 countries

Presidents and prime ministers

Here are lists of presidents of America and prime ministers of the UK.

Presidents of the United States

Date	President	Date	President
1789–97	George Washington	1881–85	Chester Arthur
1797–1801	John Adams	1885–89	Grover Cleveland
1801–09	Thomas Jefferson	1889–93	Benjamin Harrison
1809–17	James Madison	1893–97	Grover Cleveland
1817–25	James Monroe	1897–1901	William McKinley
1825–29	John Adams	1901–09	Theodore Roosevelt
1829–37	Andrew Jackson	1909–13	William H. Taft
1837–41	Martin Van Buren	1913–21	Woodrow Wilson
1841	William Henry Harrison	1921–23	Warren Harding
1841–45	John Tyler	1923–29	Calvin Coolidge
1845–49	James Polk	1929–33	Herbert Hoover
1849–50	Zachary Taylor	1933–45	Franklin D. Roosevelt
1850–53	Millard Fillmore	1945–53	Harry Truman
1853–57	Franklin Pierce	1953–61	Dwight Eisenhower
1857–61	James Buchanan	1961–63	John F. Kennedy
1861–65	Abraham Lincoln	1963–69	Lyndon Johnson
1865–69	Andrew Johnson	1969–74	Richard Nixon
1869–77	Ulysses S. Grant	1974–77	Gerald Ford
1877–81	Rutherford B. Hayes	1977–81	Jimmy Carter
1881	James Garfield	1981–89	Ronald Reagan

Date	President	Date	President
1989–93	George H.W. Bush	2001–09	George W. Bush
1993–2001	William J. Clinton	2009–	Barack Obama

Prime ministers of the United Kingdom

Date	Prime minister
1721–42	Sir Robert Walpole
1742–43	Spencer Compton, Earl of Wilmington
1743–54	Henry Pelham
1754–56	Thomas Pelham-Holles, Duke of Newcastle
1756–57	William Cavendish, Duke of Devonshire
1757	James Waldegrave, 2nd Earl Waldegrave
1757–62	Thomas Pelham Holles, Duke of Newcastle
1762–63	John Stuart, Earl of Bute
1763–65	George Grenville
1765–66	Charles Wentworth, Marquess of Rockingham
1766–68	Earl of Chatham, William Pitt "The Elder"
1768–70	Augustus Henry Fitzroy, Duke of Grafton
1770–82	Lord North
1782	Charles Wentworth, Marquess of Rockingham
1782–83	William Petty, Earl of Shelburne
1783	William Henry Cavendish Bentinck, 3rd Duke of Portland
1783–1801	William Pitt "The Younger"
1801–04	Henry Addington
1804–06	William Pitt "The Younger"
1806–07	William Wyndam Grenville, Lord Grenville
1807–09	William Henry Cavendish Bentinck, 3rd Duke of Portland
1809–12	Spencer Perceval
1812–27	Robert Banks Jenkinson, Earl of Liverpool
1827	George Canning
1827–28	Frederick Robinson, Viscount Goderich
1828–30	Arthur Wellesley, Duke of Wellington
1830–34	Earl Grey
1834	William Lamb, Viscount Melbourne
1834–35	Sir Robert Peel
1835–41	William Lamb, Viscount Melbourne

Date	Prime minister
1841–46	Sir Robert Peel
1846–52	Earl Russell
1852	Earl of Derby
1852–55	Earl of Aberdeen
1855–58	Viscount Palmerston
1858–59	Earl of Derby
1859–65	Viscount Palmerston
1865–66	Earl Russell
1866–68	Earl of Derby
1868	Benjamin Disraeli
1868–74	William Ewart Gladstone
1874–80	Benjamin Disraeli
1880–85	William Ewart Gladstone
1885–86	Robert Arthur Talbot Gascoyne-Cecil, Marquess of Salisbury
1886	William Ewart Gladstone
1886–92	Robert Arthur Talbot Gascoyne-Cecil, Marquess of Salisbury
1892–94	William Ewart Gladstone
1894–95	Earl of Rosebery
1895–1902	Robert Arthur Talbot Gascoyne-Cecil, Marquess of Salisbury
1902–05	Arthur James Balfour
1905–08	Sir Henry Campbell-Bannerman
1908–16	Herbert Henry Asquith
1916–22	David Lloyd George
1922–23	Andrew Bonar Law
1923	Stanley Baldwin
1924	James Ramsay MacDonald
1924–29	Stanley Baldwin
1929–35	James Ramsay MacDonald
1935–37	Stanley Baldwin
1937–40	Neville Chamberlain
1940–45	Sir Winston Churchill
1945–51	Clement Richard Attlee
1951–55	Sir Winston Churchill

Date	Prime minister
1955–57	Sir Anthony Eden
1957–63	Harold Macmillan
1963–64	Sir Alec Douglas-Home
1964–70	Harold Wilson
1970–74	Edward Heath
1974–76	Harold Wilson
1976–79	James Callaghan
1979–90	Margaret Thatcher
1990–97	John Major
1997–2007	Tony Blair
2007–10	Gordon Brown
2010–	David Cameron

Presidents of the European Commission

Date	President
1958–67	Walter Hallstein
1967–70	Jean Rey
1970–72	Franco Maria Malfatti
1972–3	Sicco Mansholt
1973–7	François-Xavier Ortoli
1977–81	Roy Jenkins
1981–5	Gaston Thorn
1985–95	Jacques Delors
1995–9	Jacques Santer
1999	Manuel Marín
1999–2004	Romano Prodi
2004–14	José Manuel Barroso
2014–	Jean-Claude Juncker

Proofreading

Look for errors in the following categories:

1 "Typos", which include misspelt words, punctuation mistakes, wrong numbers and transposed words or sentences.
2 Bad word breaks.
3 Layout mistakes: wrongly positioned text (including captions,

headings, folios, running heads) or illustrations, incorrect line spacing, missing items, widows (the last word of a paragraph going to another line), orphans (even worse, part of the last word going to another line).

4   Wrong fonts: errors in the use of italic, bold, typeface (eg, Arial not Times New Roman), etc.

If the text contains cross-references to numbered pages or illustrations, the proofreader is often responsible for inserting the correct reference at page-proof stage, and for checking cross-references.

The most effective way of proofreading is to read the text several times, each time with a different aim in mind, rather than attempting to carry out all checks in one go.

proofreading marks   are illustrated on pages 254–6. (The full set of proofreading marks is defined by British Standard BS 5261 "Copy preparation and proof correction".) The intention of these marks is to identify, precisely and concisely, the nature of an error and the correction required. When corrections are extensive or complex, it is usually better to spell out in full the correct form of the text rather than leave the typesetter to puzzle over a string of hieroglyphs, however immaculately drawn and ordered. Mark all proof corrections clearly and write them in the margin.

word breaks   It may be necessary to break words, using a hyphen, at the end of lines. Computer word-processing programs come with standard hyphenation rules but these can always be changed or overruled. Ideally, the aim should be to make these breaks as undisruptive as possible, so that the reader does not stumble or falter. Whenever possible, the word should be broken so that, helped by the context, the reader can anticipate the whole word from the part of it given before the break. Here are some useful principles for deciding how to break a word.

1   Words that are already hyphenated should be broken at the hyphen, not given a second hyphen.
2   Words can be broken according to either their derivation (the British convention) or their pronunciation (the US

convention): thus, *aristo-cracy* (UK) or *aristoc-racy* (US), *melli-fluous* (UK) or *mellif-luous* (US). (*See* Part 2 for American usage.)

3   Words of one syllable should not be broken.

4   Words of five or fewer characters should not be broken.

5   At least three characters must be taken over to the next line.

6   Words should not be broken so that their identity is confused or their identifying sound is distorted: thus, avoid *fun-dament, the-rapist.*

7   Personal names and acronyms (eg, NATO) should not be broken.

8   Figures should not be broken or separated from their unit of measurement.

9   A word formed with a prefix or suffix should be broken at that point: thus, *bi-furcated, ante-diluvian, convert-ible.*

10 If a breakable word contains a double consonant, split it at that point: thus, *as-sess, ship-ping, prob-lem.*

11 Do not hyphenate the last word on the right-hand page.

on-screen proofreading Proofreaders are increasingly being asked to proofread on screen, and there are various ways of doing this.

1   Print out the document or pdf, mark it up in the usual way, then scan it and save as a pdf to return by e-mail.

2   Mark up the pdf using the editing tools in a program such as Adobe Acrobat. This can be done in the traditional way with a graphics tablet, using the pen to add proofreading marks, missing letters, and so on. Missing words or phrases, comments and queries can be typed in text or comments boxes or directly onto the pdf using the typewriter tool (available in Adobe Acrobat version 7 onwards). If the creator has "enabled" the pdf, it is possible to mark up changes and add comments using Adobe Acrobat Reader (version 8 onwards).

3   Mark up a text file (in, for example, Microsoft Word) using track changes. Changes and insertions are highlighted in a different colour, deletions and formatting changes are listed in the margin, and you can add comments and queries using the Comments facility.

INSTRUCTION	TEXTUAL MARK	MARGINAL MARK AND NOTES
Correction is concluded	None	Mark after each correction. Use the circled number to indicate the number of times the same change occurs in the same line without interruption.
Leave unchanged	• • • • • under characters to remain	✓ (circled)
Insert in text the matter indicated in the margin	∧ (caret mark)	New matter followed by or
Delete	/ through character(s) or ⊢——⊣ through words	
Delete and close up space	/ through character(s) or ⊢——⊣ through words	
Close up – delete space	⌣⌢	⌣⌢
Substitute character or substitute part of one or more words	through character / or ⊢——/ through all characters	new character or new characters
Wrong font. Replace with correct font	Circle character(s) to be changed	⊗
Set in or change to italic	——— under character(s) to be set or changed	⊔

254

INSTRUCTION	TEXTUAL MARK	MARGINAL MARK AND NOTES
Set in or change to capital letters	under character(s) to be set or changed	
Set in or change to small capital letters	under character(s) to be set or changed	
Set in or change to bold type	under character(s) to be set or changed	
Set in or change to bold italic type	under character(s) to be set or changed	
Change capital letters to lower case letters	Circle character(s) to be changed	or *l.c.*
Change italic to upright type	Circle character(s) to be changed	or *roman*
Turn type or figure	Circle type or figure to be altered. Use circled number to indicate the number of degrees of rotation.	180
Substitute or insert character in superior position	through character or where required	or under character eg
Substitute or insert full stop or decimal point	through character or where required	
Substitute or insert comma	through character or where required	

INSTRUCTION	TEXTUAL MARK	MARGINAL MARK AND NOTES
Substitute or insert colon	/ through character or ⟨ where required	⊙
Substitute or insert hyphen	/ through character or ⟨ where required	⊢-⊣
Substitute or insert semi-colon	/ through character or ⟨ where required	;
Insert or substitute space	⟨ or /	⟩
Make space equal	| between words or letters	⟩
Reduce space	↑| between words or letters	↑
Start new paragraph	⌐	⌐
Run on (no new paragraph)	∽	∽
Transpose characters or words	⌐⌐ between characters or words, numbered when necessary	⌐⌐
Transpose lines	⊐	⊐
Indent	⊏	⊏
Move to the left	|←[xxxx]	⌐
Insert single or double quotes	⟨ where required	⸲ ⸲ ⸲⸲ ⸲⸲

Roman numerals

I	1	XX	20
II	2	XXI	21
III	3	XXX	30
IV	4	XL	40
V	5	L	50
VI	6	LX	60
VII	7	XC	90
VIII	8	C	100
IX	9	CC	200
X	10	D	500
XI	11	DCC	700
XII	12	DCCXIX	719
XIII	13	CM	900
XIV	14	M	1000
XV	15	MC	1100
XVI	16	MCX	1110
XVII	17	MCMXCI	1991
XVIII	18	MM	2000
XIX	19	MMX	2010

S

Solar system

	Distance from the sun			Diameter (equatorial)		
	au^a	km (m)	mi (m)	relative to Earth (=1)	km ('000)	mi ('000)
Sun	0	0	0	109.00	1,392.140	865.040
Mercury	0.39	58	36	0.38	4.880	3.032
Venus	0.72	108	67	0.95	12.103	7.520
Earth	1	150[b]	93[b]	1	12.756	7.926
Moon	–	150	93	0.27	3.475	2.159
Mars	1.52	228	142	0.53	6.794	4.221
Jupiter	5.20	778	483	11.21	142.984	88.846
Saturn	9.54	1,429	888	9.45	120.536	74.898
Uranus	19.19	2,875	1,786	4.00	51.118	31.763
Neptune	30.07	4,504	2,798	3.89	49.600	30.820

a Astronomical unit, roughly equal to the mean distance between Earth and the sun, approximately 150m km or 93m miles.

b Or 8.3 light minutes. Average distance; for the Earth the perihelion distance (at the point nearest to the sun) is 147.1×10^6 km = 91.4×10^6 mi = 8.2 light minutes, and the aphelion distance (at the point furthest from the sun) is 153.1×10^6 km = 95.1×10^6 mi = 8.5 light minutes.

Note: Pluto used to be included as one of the planets in the solar system, but it was downgraded in 2006. Some astronomers disagree with this decision.

Technology abbreviations

Here is a list of commonly used technology abbreviations.

ADSL	asymmetric digital subscriber line
AOL	America Online
ASCII	American standard code for information interchange
ASP	application service provider (or active server page)
BCC	blind carbon copy
BPS	bits per second
CAD	computer-aided design
CC	carbon copy
CDMA	code-division multiple access
CPC	cost per click
CSS	cascading style sheets (or client-security software)
CGI	common gateway interface (or computer-generated imagery)
COM	component object model
DES	data-encryption standard
DHCP	dynamic host configuration protocol
DHTML	dynamic hypertext mark-up language
DNS	domain-name system
DRM	digital-rights management
DSL	digital subscriber line (or loop)
EDI	electronic data interchange
EFF	electronic frontier foundation
FAQ	frequently asked questions
FDM	frequency-division multiplexing
FSF	free software foundation

FTP	file transfer protocol
GIF	graphics interchange format
GPRS	general packet radio service
GSM	global system for mobile communications
GUI	graphical user interface
HTML	hypertext mark-up language
HTTP	hypertext transfer protocol
IAB	internet architecture board
IANA	internet assigned-numbers authority
ICANN	internet corporation for assigned names and numbers
ICQ	I seek you
IDS	intrusion-detection system
IETF	internet engineering task-force
IM	instant messaging
IMAP	internet message-access protocol
IOT	internet of things
IP	internet protocol
IPTV	internet protocol television
IRC	internet relay chat
IRL	in real life
ISDN	integrated services digital network
ISP	internet service provider
JANET	joint academic network
JPEG	joint photographic experts group (or JPG)
KBPS	kilobits per second
LAN	local-area network
LDAP	lightweight directory access protocol
LINX	London internet exchange
LTE	long-term evolution
MBPS	megabits (millions of bits) per second
MIME	multi-purpose internet mail extensions
MMS	multimedia messaging service
MOO	multi-user domain (MUD), object oriented
MPEG	moving-picture experts group
NAP	network access point
NCSA	National Centre for Supercomputing Applications
NNTP	network-news transfer protocol

OFDM	orthogonal frequency-division multiplexing
OS	open source/operating system
OSI	open-source initiative
P2P	peer to peer
PAAS	platform as a service
PCS	personal communications service
PDA	personal digital assistant
PDF	portable document format
PGP	pretty good privacy
PHP	hypertext preprocessor
PKI	public key infrastructure
POP	point of presence
POP3	post-office protocol (latest version)
POTS	plain old telephone service
PPP	point-to-point protocol
QOS	quality of service
RDF	resource-description framework
RFC	request for comments
RSS	really simple syndication (or rich site summary)
SAAS	software as a service
SMS	short message service
SMTP	simple mail-transport protocol
SOAP	simple object access protocol
SQL	structured query language
SSL	secure sockets layer
TCP	transmission-control protocol
TCP/IP	transmission-control protocol/internet protocol
TD-SCDMA	time-division synchronous code-division multiple access
TDM	time-division multiplexing
TLA	three-letter acronym
TLD	top-level domain
TTP	trusted third party
UC	unified communications
UDDI	universal description, discovery and integration
UDRP	uniform domain-name dispute-resolution policy
UMTS	universal mobile-telecommunications system
URI	uniform resource identifier

URL	uniform resource locator
UTF	unicode transformation format
UUCP	unix-to-unix copy protocol
UWB	ultra-wideband
VM	virtual machine
VOD	video-on-demand
VOIP	voice-over IP
VPN	virtual private network
VRML	virtual-reality modelling language
W3C	world wide web consortium
WAN	wide area network
WAP	wireless-application protocol
WASP	wireless-application service provider
W-CDMA	wideband code-division multiple access
WDM	wavelength-division multiplexing
WEP	wired equivalent privacy
WIMAX	worldwide interoperability for microwave access
WLAN	wireless local area network
WMA	windows media audio
WML	wireless mark-up language
WPA	Wi-Fi protected access
WPAN	wireless personal area network
WSDL	web services description language
WWW	world wide web
XHTML	extensible hypertext mark-up language
XML	extensible mark-up language
XRBL	extensible business-reporting language
XSL	extensible stylesheet language

Time of day around the world

Here is a list of countries of the world showing how many hours
fast (+) or slow (–) they are relative to Greenwich Mean Time (GMT).
The figures show the winter clock time; where summer time is
normally observed, the hour is marked with*.

Algeria +1	Australia	Tasmania, Victoria
Angola +1	New South Wales,	+10*
Argentina –3	Canberra,	Queensland +10

South Australia
+9.5*
Northern Territory
+9.5
Western Australia
+8
Austria +1*
Azerbaijan +4*
Bahamas -5*
Bahrain +3
Bangladesh +6
Belarus +2*
Belgium +1*
Bolivia -4
Brazil
  Fernando de
    Noronha -2
  Coast & Brasilia -3*
  West -4*
  Acre -5
Brunei +8
Bulgaria +2*
Canada
  Newfoundland
    Island -3.5*
  Atlantic -4*
  Eastern -5*
  Central -6*
  Mountain -7*
  Pacific -8*
Chile -4*
China (mainland) +8*
Colombia -5
Congo
  Katanga, Kivu +2
  Kinshasa +1
Costa Rica -6
Croatia +1*

Cyprus +2*
Czech Republic +1*
Denmark +1*
Dominican Republic
  -4
Ecuador -5
Egypt +2*
Estonia +2*
Ethiopia +3
Finland +2*
France +1*
Germany +1*
Ghana GMT
Greece +2*
Hong Kong +8
Hungary+1*
Iceland GMT
India +5.5
Indonesia
  Eastern +9
  Central +8
  Western +7
Iran +3.5*
Iraq +3*
Ireland GMT
Israel +2*
Italy +1*
Ivory Coast GMT
Jamaica -5
Japan +9
Kazakhstan (West) +4
  Aktau, Atyrau,
    Aktyubinsk,
    Uralsk +5
  Almaty, Astana +6
Kenya +3
Korea, North & South
  +9

Kuwait +3
Latvia +2*
Lebanon +2*
Libya +2
Lithuania +2*
Luxembourg +1*
Malaysia +8
Malta +1*
Mexico, Mexico City
  -6*
Morocco GMT
Netherlands +1*
New Zealand +12*
Nigeria +1
Norway +1*
Oman +4
Pakistan +5
Panama -5
Papua New Guinea
  +10
Paraguay -4*
Peru -5
Philippines +8
Poland +1*
Portugal GMT*
Puerto Rico -4
Qatar +3
Romania +2*
Russia
  Moscow +3*
  Omsk +6*
Saudi Arabia +3
Serbia and
  Montenegro +1*
Sierra Leone GMT
Singapore +8
Slovakia +1*
Slovenia +1*

South Africa +2 Turkey +2* Pacific −8*
Spain +1* Ukraine +2* Alaska −9*
Sweden +1* United Arab Emirates Hawaii −10
Switzerland +1* +4 Uruguay −3
Syria +2* United Kingdom Uzbekistan +5
Taiwan +8 GMT* Venezuela −4
Tajikistan +5 United States Vietnam +7
Thailand +7 Eastern −5* Yemen +3
Trinidad & Tobago −4 Central −6* Zambia +2
Tunisia +1 Mountain −7* Zimbabwe +2

Index